Index to Fabulous Book Arts

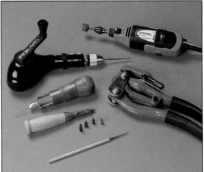

Cutting Tools
Craft knives • X-Acto knife • Fiskars paper trimmers

Hole Punching Tools
Dremel tool • Awls • Japanese screw punch • Hand drill

Applicators • Folders • Boards
Foam brushes • Brayer • Bristle brushes • Bone folders • Cutting boards

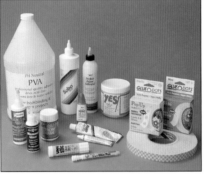

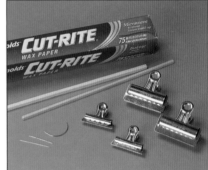

Rulers
Metal T-square • Quilter's ruler • Aluminum ruler with recessed foam backing

Adhesives
Glue sticks • PVA • Sobo • Yes! • E6000 • Gem-Tac • Quick Grab • Double-stick tape

Helpful Extras
Waxed paper • Binder clips • Square dowels • Needles

Bookbinding Tools

While it isn't necessary to possess every tool known to the craft, it is helpful to have a few basics to make the art go smoothly. These can be broken down into a few categories: cutting and shaping tools, rulers, bone folders, and needles.

Cutting and Shaping Tools

The most important of these is a good, sharp craft knife. These come in a variety of shapes and sizes. My favorite is the type with snap-off blades. I prefer this type because a fresh blade is always at hand and they are inexpensive to replace. A sharp blade is important for two reasons: to get a clean edge on the material you're cutting and to prevent injuries. When your blade is dull, you're much more likely to slip and cut yourself. Replace your blades often.

The question I get in class most often is, "How do you cut book board?" I prefer a Fiskars hand-held rotary cutter. It slices through even the thickest board with ease.

For cutting whole reams of paper, unless you want to invest in a guillotine paper cutter, (which can run into the thousands of dollars) you can't beat a local print shop. They can usually do the job for just a few dollars while you wait. If you're cutting a few sheets at a time, I like the Fiskars desk rotary cutter. It comes in 12" and 24" models and is fairly precise, provided it's used properly. (When cutting, it's important to put one hand on the paper you're cutting to prevent it from sliding away from the blade.) I like this model because the blades and cutting surface are easily replaced when they wear out.

For miscellaneous cutting, drilling, sanding and finishing jobs, a Dremel tool is an excellent investment. This crafter's tool is found in hardware stores and comes with a myriad of attachments. The tools come in both cordless and corded models. If your budget only allows you one, I would choose a corded model since it affords more power, and nothing is more frustrating than waiting to finish a project while a battery recharges.

An awl is a sharp tool used for poking holes. They come in many sizes, so be sure to use a thin one so that your holes are the correct size. Also, be careful when using a graduated type that you don't make the hole too big by pushing too far. I prefer to use a jeweler's awl, because the needle is long and sharp. The handle and the needle are made of one piece of metal, so the needle won't come loose.

Many different types of hole-punching tools are available. I use a variety of them, but my favorite is the Japanese Screw Punch. This tool is basically a self-contained anywhere hole punch. It's lightweight and compact, and comes with bits ranging from 1 mm to 4 mm size holes. It can punch a hole in several sheets of paper at a time, and can punch through matboard, book board, craft metal and metal mesh. Its best feature is that it's not limited by the reach of traditional hole punches.

While we're talking about cutting tools, I should mention that a cutting board is an essential tool. They prevent damage to both your work surface and cutting blade. Choose the appropriate size for your needs and keep it on your work surface at all times. Most models have a 1" grid that can also be helpful in measuring and cutting on a 90-degree angle.

1. Apply adhesive to one side of board. Place face down, centered on larger piece of cover paper.

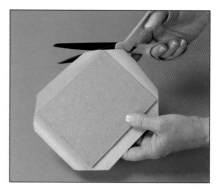

2. Miter all four corners, leaving a piece equal to the height of the board in each corner.

3. Put adhesive on one flap. Fold over, press into place, burnish with waxed paper. Press corner down using bone folder. Repeat for remaining three flaps.

4. Apply adhesive to smaller piece of cover paper.

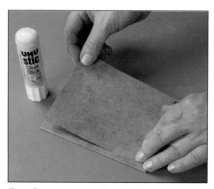

5. Center and adhere cover paper to the book board. Let dry completely.

Rulers

There are quite a few rulers that can do simple jobs well. I have a favorite that one of my students introduced me to a couple of years ago: a quilter's ruler. Olfa and Fiskars make two of the more common models. If I had a preference, it would be the Olfa brand because the yellow markings are easy on the eyes. This ruler comes in a variety of lengths and widths and it's the width that makes it so helpful. It enables you to measure and cut at the same time. If you don't have one, find one in a sewing notions department and ask a knowledgeable clerk to show you how it works. You'll be sold.

The only thing that is not ideal about a quilter's ruler is that since it's transparent by design, it can slip while you're cutting if you're not careful. If this is a problem for you, choose any of a variety of metal-edged rulers with a cork or foam backing. The drafting department of a craft store usually has an assortment. That's where I found my favorite: an aluminum ruler with recessed foam backing that allows the ruler to lie completely flush with the work surface. This feature prevents your knife from slipping under the edge of the ruler.

For heavy jobs such as cutting large pieces of book board, a long metal T square is necessary. The advantage of this type of ruler over a standard straightedge is that the T helps you attain a 90-degree angle more easily when you match it to the markings on a cutting mat.

Bone Folders

A bone folder is a polymer-plastic tool made for scoring paper to make clean folds. It comes in a variety of lengths, sizes and shapes. I prefer a curved type with a thin flat tip that ends in a sharp point. It fits nicely in the hand and its thinly honed edge makes crisp folds in papers.

Needles

Needles used in bookbinding are somewhat different than sewing needles. Ideally, they should have a slightly larger eye to accommodate heavy waxed linen threads but not so large as to widen the holes of the signature, thereby compromising the integrity of the structure. (Rather than using large-eyed needles, flatten the end of the thread.) Binder's needles tend to be slightly longer than sewing needles. This helps to get into tight spaces. I prefer round-tipped needles to sharps because I'm accident-prone. If your bookbinding needles are sharps, you can easily sand the tip off with sand paper or a Dremel tool. Some binders prefer curved needles, but I haven't found a stitch yet that requires one.

Other items I find useful that don't really fall into a particular category are waxed paper and blank newsprint. A wad of waxed paper acts as a great burnishing tool for covering book board and other glue tasks. It moves smoothly over the surface, removing wrinkles and flattening the paper without leaving marks. I work on a newsprint pad. It protects my work surface from inks, stains and glues. When one page is used, just tear it off and you have a fresh surface.

Adhesives

Another common question I hear in class is, "How do you know what type of glue to use for a particular job?" The short answer to that question is "The least type of glue needed for the job." What does that mean? Glues can be classified in a number of ways, but I prefer to classify them in terms of stickiness. In other words, use only the level of stickiness necessary for the job. For the purposes of this book, I will only cover adhesives I use on a regular basis. However, there are many more on the market that will do different jobs well.

Level 1:

Glue stick - paper to cardstock, assuming it doesn't have to bear weight. Examples: Gluing two pages together or covering book board with thin paper. The advantage of a glue stick is that it's a fairly easy and dry application. This means less wrinkling or distortion of the paper. The disadvantage is that this type of glue is not as strong as others. So if you ask it to adhere a heavy paper or stand up to repeated openings and closings, it may fail. Keep the cap on when not in use or it may become too sticky to glide smoothly. I prefer the purple Uhu glue stick for its smoothness and the purple color (which dries clear) is helpful to see where you've applied it.

Level 2:

PVA - Polyvinyl acetate is a smooth white adhesive that dries clear. It's useful for binding heavy papers, boards or fabrics together. It will bear some weight but not heavy objects. I like to tell students that the biggest advantage is that it dries much faster than other white glues, and its biggest disadvantage is that it dries much faster than other white glues. In other words, if you know what you're doing and are focused, deliberate and steady, you'll love the speed with which this glue allows you to work. If you tend to make placement errors, it can be unforgiving. In the latter case, Sobo glue might be a better choice for you as it dries somewhat slower, allowing you the opportunity to rearrange at times. In either case, I suggest applying this type of glue with a soft bristle brush or sponge brush. It can be helpful to dip your brush in water before the glue to thin it a bit and allow your brush to flow more smoothly. For large areas, a sponge brayer can be a great tool since it puts on a thin, even layer very quickly. For small areas, I've been known to apply it with my finger because I'm too impatient to search for a brush.

Level 3:

Dimensional Adhesive - This type of adhesive is useful for adhering dimensional objects of varying sizes. It typically takes much longer to dry depending on the amount used and the size of the object to be adhered. A few examples are Gem-Tac, E6000 and Quick Grab. My favorite in this group is Gem-Tac for its inoffensive odor. Another recent addition to this list is a product called Glue Dots. These are small dabs of a very sticky adhesive that come on a paper roll. They come in several sizes. Surprisingly strong considering their size, they can hold small objects such as coins or charms with ease. Keep your fingers away from them, as they can be hard to remove.

Keep in mind that there are other methods for adhering heavy objects such as wiring or tying objects in place. If glue isn't doing the trick, consider another angle.

Preparing Signatures

1. Fold text sheets in half one at a time. Press the sheets flat with a bone folder.

2. Nest in groups (signatures) per project instructions. Mark a T in pencil in the top right corner of each to signify the tops.

3. Prepare a punching pattern (jig) per project instructions.

4. Nest the jig inside the signature and punch holes with an awl according to pattern. Use a Davey board cradle if you have one or punch by hand.

1. Place ribbon in the center fold of a signature of paper.

2. Tie each signature around the spine with ribbon and a bow. We used 3 signatures.

Memories of Paris

*S*heer ribbons tie the signatures into this book, and provide a lovely spine accent as well. Decorate with mementos from a trip abroad, or embellish with found objects representing a faraway land.

SIZE: 4" x 5"

MATERIALS:
2 pieces book board 4" x 5"
1 piece spine board 1" x 4"
1 piece cover paper 7" x 12"
1 piece end paper 9" x 4$^{1}/8$"
3 pieces ribbon 20"

1 piece ribbon 6"
18 pieces text paper 4$^{1}/8$" x 7"
1 brass button
2 plastic buttons
6" brown waxed linen thread
Various collage materials

This is a Great Beginner Project !

sample created by Kristen Badowski

SUPPLIES:
Ruler • Glue stick • Bone folder • Awl • French-themed rubber stamps • Black *Marvy* ink pad • Chestnut *Colorbox* Cat's Eye ink pad • Double-stick mounting tape • $^{3}/16$" wooden spacer • Waxed paper • Floss or thread

INSTRUCTIONS:
Lay cover paper face down horizontally on work space. Draw 1" margins on left side of paper and bottom edge. Apply glue stick to first cover board and lay in corner where two lines meet. Burnish cover paper with wad of waxed paper. Lay spacer to right of cover board. Apply glue stick to spine board and lay next to spacer. Burnish. Remove spacer and lay next to spine board. Glue other cover board into place next to spacer. Remove spacer. Miter corners. Apply glue stick to flaps and wrap paper around cover boards one at a time. Burnish each one. Apply glue stick to other cover paper and use to cover inside of cover assembly. Burnish well.

Fold text papers in half to form sheets 3$^{1}/2$" x 4$^{1}/8$". Nest into three signatures of 6 sheets each. Loop ribbon through first signature and tie to spine with bow on outside of spine. Repeat for other two signatures. Stagger the bows on spine.

Arrange collage materials on front cover and attach items with glue stick or double-stick mounting tape. Stamp with French rubber stamps.

Use awl to make hole in front cover, centered about $^{1}/2$" from right edge. Attach brass button to outside of cover with brown waxed linen thread using plastic button on inside of cover. Make hole on back cover in same position as front cover. Thread ribbon ends through hole from outside of cover and through holes in remaining plastic button. Adjust loop so it fits over cover button. Knot ends through holes in button.

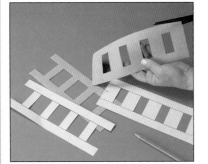

1. Cut hinge templates.

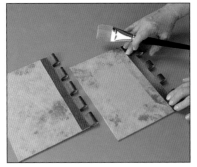

2. Glue hinges to front and back covers.

3. Punch sewing holes using awl and jig.

4. Sew signatures to spine.

5. Glue spine to covers.

Continued on page 10.

Atlas' Secret

*T*he secret to this book is in the hinge - simply fit the front and back together, and slide a decorated dowel pin into place to hold them together.

SIZE: 7¹/4" x 9"
MATERIALS:
2 pieces book board 6¹/2" x 9"
2 pieces cover paper 10" x 13"
Burgundy vinyl for hinge
8¹/2" x 2¹/2" cardstock for sewing jig
1 dowel ¹/2" round x 9"
Dowel cover art

9 sheets Ancient Gold parchment text paper
Map for spine piece
Front and back cover art
Front and back end papers
3 pieces 18" Yellow waxed linen thread
1 eye pin
Beads and fibers for dowel embellishment

SUPPLIES:
X-Acto knife • Cutting mat • Metal-edged ruler • Scissors • Jewelry pliers • Wire cutters • Awl • Glue stick • PVA glue • Glue brush • Bone folder • Binder's needle • Metallic rub-ons • Dabber • Super glue

Covering the book boards:

Apply glue stick to entire side of one piece of book board. Lay face down on wrong side of cover paper. Miter corners with scissors, leaving an amount of paper at corner equal to thickness of board. Apply glue stick to one side and fold paper over. Burnish flat with bone folder or a wad of waxed paper. Repeat for opposite side. Then do other two sides in same manner. Repeat for other book board. Pick short side on each board and designate top by marking a T in pencil on inside.

Making the hinges:

Measure circumference of hinge pin by wrapping a string around it. Add ¹/4" to that measurement to calculate barrel width. Decide how much hinge material you want overlapping your cover. Multiply that by two, and add barrel width. This is your hinge width. Height of hinge is usually equal to height of book. Decide how many barrels you want in your hinge (an odd number) and divide height of your hinge by that number. This will be height of each barrel. Barrels need not all be same height.

Cut out hinge template using X-Acto knife and ruler. Trace both patterns on wrong side of vinyl and label tops of each with T to match template. Cut out vinyl hinges with scissors. Round corners if desired.

Adhering the hinges:

Pick board you want to be back cover. Take hinge that resembles ladder and lay face down T on top. Draw bead of PVA glue down right side of hinge. With glue brush, spread along that side, taking care not to go into barrel area of hinge. Once glue is spread, set back cover on it face down so that T on cover is oriented the same as T on hinge.

Check to see that the two pieces are aligned properly. Set that assembly aside and put heavy book on top to weight down. • Take other hinge and lay it face down in front of you with T facing up. Apply glue evenly along left side. Place front cover on it. Set aside and put a heavy book on it to weight down.

Take back cover with hinge partially attached and apply glue down left side of hinge. Use glue brush to spread glue to edges. Wrap hinge around opposite side of cover so only barrels protrude. Hold in place for a minute until glue begins to set. Set aside and place a heavy book on top to weight down. Repeat procedure for front cover. Allow glue to set.

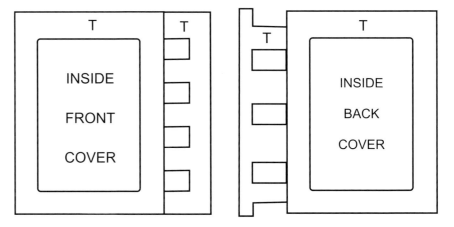

samples created by Lisa Renner

Dowels and hinges are one of the ways to bind your art books together. Here, fibers decorate the dowel along with beads that have been added to the fibers.

Continued from page 10.

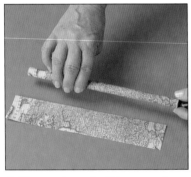

6. Cover dowel with map piece to create hinge pin.

7. Tear page edges and rub with metallics to age.

Preparing jig and signatures:

Fold 8¹/2" x 2¹/2" piece of parchment cardstock in half lengthwise to 8¹/2" x 1¹/4". On fold, make marks at the following measurements from top: 1¹/4", 2³/4", 4¹/4", 5³/4" and 7¹/4". Make a T on top of same side as sewing hole marks and fold again so sewing hole marks are on inside of jig. Set aside and prepare signatures.

Fold nine pieces of parchment paper in half to 8¹/2" x 5¹/2". Nest 3 sheets inside each other to make three signatures. Mark a T in pencil in top right corner of each signature. If you plan to leave pages straight, shorten width of signatures slightly by trimming open side of each to 5". If you plan to tear edges of pages, skip this step.

Preparing accordion fold spine piece:

Cut map piece 8¹/2" square. Fold piece in half vertically with right sides together. Fold each half in half again from edges to center, right sides together, to make four panels. Fold each panel in half again, this time in opposite direction. This should result in a piece that looks like this from the end with the map side facing up. Double-check that your spine looks like this diagram with map side up. If not, refold to match.

Punching sewing holes:

Signatures will be sewn to accordion fold. Both sets of holes must be punched at the same time to assure they match. Nest the first signature in the first valley fold (from left) of the map. The map will be facing you as you punch. Nest the jig inside that, checking to see that the Ts of both jig and signature match up with the top of the map. Punch five holes with your awl. Nest the second signature in the second valley fold of the map with the jig inside and punch five holes.

Repeat for the last signature.

*F*ollow the diagrams shown here to bind or sew your signatures (pages nested together) to the spine piece of your book. This is a 5-hole pamphlet stitch.

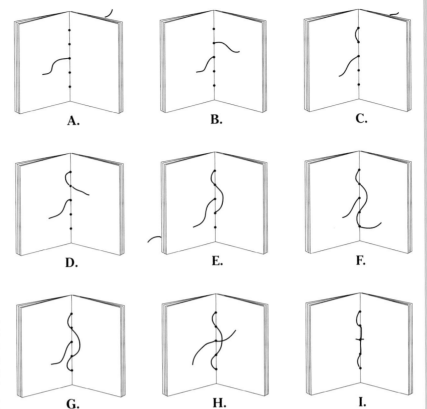

A.   B.   C.

D.   E.   F.

G.   H.   I.

Sewing signatures to spine piece:

Although you punched holes with map side facing you, signatures will be sewn to opposite side of accordion panel. Thread needle with first piece of waxed linen. Turn the spine piece of the signature you punched last so the map is facing away. Sew this signature to what is now the first mountain fold of the plain side of the spine. Align the two pieces fold to fold, with holes matching.

Refer to drawings as you stitch.

Insert threaded needle into center hole from the inside of the signature (A). Come back through the hole directly above the center (B). Go out through the top hole (C). Come back into the second hole from the top (D). Skip the center hole and go out through the hole beneath the center hole (E). Come back through the bottom hole (F). Go back through the hole below the center hole (G). Come back through the center hole (H). Tie off with a square knot and clip threads to 1/4" (I). Repeat for the other two signatures.

Assembling the book:

Apply glue to the last accordion fold and adhere to the back cover so the barrels protrude beyond the spine piece, overlapping the hinge on the inside of the cover. Smooth with a bone folder or wad of waxed paper. Repeat, adhering the front accordion panel to the front cover.

Trim end papers. Before applying glue, double-check to be sure they fit inside the covers. Trim a bit from one or both inside edges if necessary. Apply glue with a glue brush and adhere the end papers.

For an aged appearance, tear rough edges on the pages and rub with metallic rub-ons.

Finishing the dowel:

To make a hinge pin, trim map piece to the same height as dowel. Using a glue stick, adhere map to the dowel, overlapping just a bit. Be sure edges are firmly glued. Poke a small hole in the top of the dowel.

Open end of eye pin with jewelry pliers. Find center point of fibers and slide into open loop. Close loop. Adhere flat bead to top of dowel with a drop of super glue. Cut eye pin shorter to fit it into the hole. Put a bend in the eye pin to help keep it in the dowel. Before inserting it, a drop of super glue on the bend will help insure that it stays put. Drop another flat bead on top of the dowel and insert the eye pin into the hole. Insert the dowel into the hinge.

Cut out the front and back cover art. Adhere to the covers using a glue stick. If desired, stamp crackle stamp in gold randomly across both pieces to age.

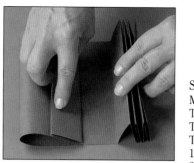

1. Fold a 16-panel accordion spine.

2. Adhere spine to front and back covers.

3. Punch holes in spine using awl and template.

4. Edge and stamp the tags as desired.

5. Insert fibers on tags into holes in spine of book.

Continued on page 14.

Tag Flag Book

SIZE: 5 1/2" x 5 1/2"

MATERIALS:
Two pieces Davey board, 5 1/2" square
Two pieces cover paper 7 1/2" square
Two pieces cover paper 5" square
1 piece Buff Canson paper 24" X 5 1/2"
2 sheets coffee-dyed tag art
1 sheet alphabetic ephemera
2 brass 1/8" eyelets, 1 red eyelet heart
1 brass brad

1 hole punching template
14 fibers, 15" each
Bead threader
6 brass crimp beads
1 drawer pull
1 antique map
1 rust tag
'Journey' typewriter letters
7 washers
1 dragonfly charm

SUPPLIES:
Glue stick • Scissors • 1/4" and 1/8" punches (helpful: 1/2", 3/8", 5/8") • Eyelet setter • Hammer • Glue dots • Double-stick mounting tape • *ColorBox* Cat's Eye (Chestnut, Rousillon) • Burnt Umber *F & W* Artist Acrylic • Awl • Assorted rubber stamps and brown ink pads • PVA glue

INSTRUCTIONS:
Preparing the cover structure:

Cover both Davey boards with cover paper using a glue stick. Miter corners and fold flaps over one pair at a time. Use 5" square cover paper to cover remainder on reverse side. Fold Canson strip into a 16-panel accordion spine. Cut off two panels of spine. Glue to inside covers so there are seven valley folds inside the open cover.

Trim hole-punching template and score on dotted line. Nest inside the first valley fold and punch top hole only. Nest in the next fold and punch both holes. Repeat for the next four valley folds. Nest inside the last fold and punch bottom hole only.

Preparing the tags:

Trim the 12 tags, punch the hole and edge each one with Chestnut Cat's Eye ink. Stamp as desired. Cut or punch each of the letters out and attach to appropriate places on the tag art using glue dots. Attach eyelets and brad. Last, attach a fiber to each tag hole. Before beginning to insert tags into book, be sure the pages are in order.

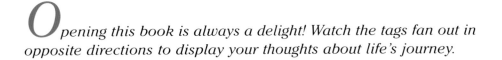

Opening this book is always a delight! Watch the tags fan out in opposite directions to display your thoughts about life's journey.

As you Journey through LIFE, choose Your DESTiNATiONs WELL,

But do NoT hurry thEre. You wiLL ARrivE sooN ENou gH.

WAndER the bAckroADS & foRgOTTEn PATHs.

& If UPON ArriVaL, you fiND thaT YouR deStinatiON is not eXAcTLy As you HaD dReAmed,

Do Not BE DiSAPPoiNTed.

tHink Of aLL you WOulD HAVE MiSSed BUT FOR tHE JOuRNEy There.

& KNow THAt tHE TRuE WoRTh OF YOUr tRAVELs

Li WhEr cAMe At

Continued from page 13.

6. Age front cover edges with ink.

7. Glue letters to washers with glue stick.

Tag Flag Book Cover

Inserting tags:

Using a bead threader, thread fibers of first tag through top hole in first valley fold. Pull thread all the way through the hole until tag is resting in the fold.

Apply PVA glue to the $1^1/4''$ of the back side of the tag near the hole and adhere it to the right side of the fold. Note: All of the top row of tags will be adhered to the right side of the valley fold and all of the bottom tags will be adhered to the left side of the fold.

Repeat this procedure for the remainder of the top row of tags, making sure that the poem reads correctly before gluing. The first tag on the bottom row will be inserted into the second valley fold. Thread the fiber through the hole and pull until the tag is snug in the fold. Apply PVA glue to front $1^1/4''$ of tag near hole and adhere to left side of second fold.

Repeat this procedure for the remaining tags.

Preparing the cover art:

Age the front cover edges with two Cat's Eyes. Tear the map out and age the edges with Chestnut Cat's Eye. Adhere it to the cover with a glue stick. Stamp the rust tag with a Judikins marble background stamp. String the remaining fibers on the tag and glue it to the map with PVA glue. Age the washers with F & W Artist Acrylic. Punch out the Journey letters and glue them to the washers with a glue stick.

Attach the washers to the tag with double stick mounting tape. Attach the dragonfly with two glue dots. Age the drawer pull with F & W Artist's Acrylic and attach it to the right side of the cover. Enjoy!

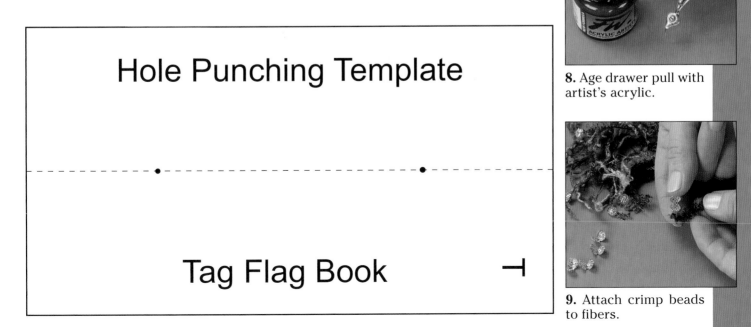

8. Age drawer pull with artist's acrylic.

9. Attach crimp beads to fibers.

Hole Punching Template

•   •

Tag Flag Book ⌐

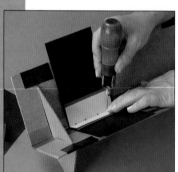

1. Punch holes in signature using an awl and jig.

2. Sew signatures with waxed linen thread.

Continued on page 18.

Chinese Star by M.K. Seckler, The Last Supper and Celtic Dreams by April Mott

This spectacular book offers plenty of pockets to hold tags, cards and tokens.

Chinese Star Book

SIZE: 3¹/2" x 5¹/2"

MATERIALS:

1 piece matboard 5¹/2" x 7"
2 pieces cover paper 5¹/2" x 7¹/2"
1 piece gold Ichizen paper 2" x 5"
Cardstock as follows:
      Layer 1: 7 pieces black 3¹/2" x 11"
      Layer 2: 7 pieces red 3" x 7"
      Layer 3: 7 pieces red 3¹/2" x 8"
      Layer 4: 7 pieces ivory 7" x 7"
1 hole punching template
1 sheet mah jongh tile art
3 sheets Chinese proverbs on ivory cardstock
1 Chinese coin
1 black screen disc with Xyron adhesive backing
Fibers for cover art
12 beads for spine decoration
1¹/2 yards black waxed linen thread
24" feet red ribbon

SUPPLIES:

PVA glue • Glue paper • Glue stick • Double-stick tape • E6000 glue • Craft knife • Cutting board • Scissors • Awl • Bone folder • 2 bookbinding needles • Two heavy-duty rubber bands or heavy weight • Various Asian writing rubber stamps • Black stamp pad • *ColorBox* Topaz Cat's Eye Ink Pad • Deckle scissors

A.

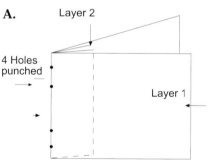

Layer 2

4 Holes punched

Layer 1

B.

Thread Center Holes
From Inside to Outside

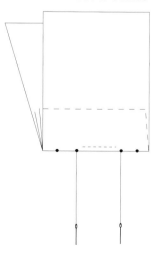

3. Glue signature cardstock back to back.

4. Glue decorated layer in place using a glue stick.

5. Glue next decorated layer in place using a glue stick.

6. Add artwork in pockets.

Preparing signatures:

Fold layer 1 in half to create seven folded sheets measuring 3½" x 5½". Fold layer 2 in half to create seven folded sheets measuring 3" x 3½". Fold these sheets in half again to create seven sheets measuring 1½" x 3½", with the long fold measuring 3½". Cut out punching template and fold it along the dotted line. Mark a T in top right corner to signify top. Nest layer 2 inside layer 1. The open (non-folded) end of layer two should be at the top so when jig is nested inside layers, the T on jig will be aligned with open end.

Punch four holes in each of the seven nested signatures (A). In sewing directions, we will refer to two middle holes as 'center holes' and first and last holes as 'end holes'.

Sewing book:

Thread waxed linen thread with a needle at each end. Beginning inside first signature, thread needles from the two center holes to the outside of the spine (B). (Fold the thread in half before threading the needles and make sure the midpoint of the thread is between the two center holes.) Cross needles and thread each one back through opposite center hole to the inside of signature.

With each needle, go directly out nearest end hole to the outside of signature (C). Add 2nd signature next to first, taking care to match open ends of red layer 2. Thread each needle into corresponding end hole of 2nd signature. Pull threads snugly to tighten, but not so tightly as to tear cardstock.

Thread each needle through nearest center hole of 2nd signature and pull to outside of spine. On 2nd, 4th and 6th signatures add four beads (2 black, 2 red in any pattern) to one needle and thread that needle through opposite center hole to inside of signature.

Thread the other needle (on the outside of spine) directly through four beads and then opposite center hole to inside of 2nd signature. Repeat from * adding signatures and beading every other signature until seven have been sewn. On odd signatures, when there is no beading, just cross threads over without adding any beads.

When the sewing is finished, tie off threads with a square knot (right over left, left over right) in center holes of inside of last signature. Affix ribbons to the book block with double-stick tape.

Chinese Star by M. K. Seckler

Continued from page 17.

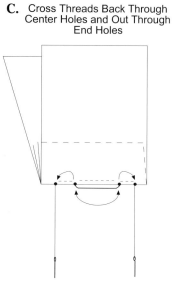

C. Cross Threads Back Through Center Holes and Out Through End Holes

7. Affix the ribbon to the book block using double-stick tape.

8. Attach covers with PVA glue or Tombow adhesive.

9. Decorate the cover.

Assembling book:

Notice that when you close the book so that the beads show on the spine, two pieces of black cardstock are back to back in six places. Glue these layers together where they meet using a glue stick. Be careful not to get glue anywhere but these sheets. Wrap a heavy-duty rubber band around each end or place the book block under a heavy weight and set aside.

Cut matboard in half to make 2 pieces $3^1/2$" x $5^1/2$". Cover matboards with two pieces of cover paper. Miter corners to reduce thickness.

For front cover, adhere gold Momi paper vertically and to left of center using a glue stick. Wrap extra around and adhere to wrong side. Cut ribbon in half. Double-stick tape one ribbon to inside of one of short sides of each cover.

Using PVA glue or Tombow Multi glue, adhere covers to book block, making sure ribbons are on open side of book and not spine side.

Align covers and replace rubber bands or weight to set the glue.

Celtic Dreams by April Mott

The Last Supper by April Mott

HOLE PUNCHING TEMPLATE

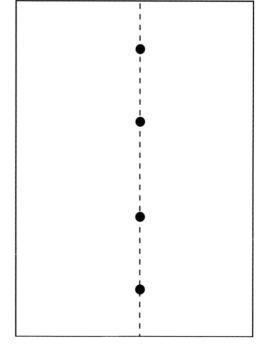

Fold layer 3 in half to create seven layers measuring 3¹/2"
x 4". Stamp insides of sheets with Asian writing stamp if
desired. Remove rubber bands from book block. Apply glue
stick to each 3¹/2" edge of layer 3 pieces and insert each into
one open signature.

Glue only the edges of the insert to the edges of each signature to form a star. Repeat for remaining six signatures. Be
sure there is no glue showing and replace rubber bands or
weight. • Fold layer 4 in half to create 7 layers measuring 3¹/2"
x 7". Stamp the top half of the inside of each folded panel. Tear
or cut unstamped side in either one horizontal line or two diag-
onal lines.

Fold layer again to 3¹/2" square. Open layer and stamp out-
sides of each folded pocket if desired. Brush edges with Topaz
Cat's Eye to age.

Apply glue stick to each 3¹/2" edge of folded pockets.
Insert one into each of seven open pages. Be sure there is no
glue showing and replace rubber bands or weight.

Trim 14 (7 left facing and 7 right facing) pocket inserts
(proverbs) with straight or deckle scissors. Trim mah jongh
tiles and glue to each insert. Edge with Topaz Cat's Eye. Put
inserts into each pocket. Tie ribbons to close. To finish cover
art, peel the Xyron backing off screen and adhere screen to gold
Momi paper. Attach fibers with slipknot through center of coin.
Glue coin to screen using E6000.

1. Roll paper bead using black, then gold paper.

2. Wrap wire and seed beads around paper bead. Brush with Diamond Glaze. Glue bead to a painted bamboo skewer.

3. Trim the cover templates. Score and cut the cover cardstock.

4. Prepare the cover art. Attach closure loop on left flap and Asian tissue and coin on the right.

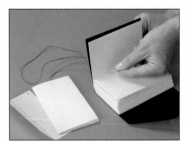

5. Fold and nest signatures. Sew into cover with waxed linen thread.
Continued on page 22.

Continued on page 22.

INSTRUCTIONS:

Preparing closure: Paint one skewer with red acrylic paint. When dry, roll over Asian writing stamp inked with Black Brilliance or Fabrico ink. Roll a strip of black paper tightly onto the center of the other skewer. After completing one or two revolutions, apply glue stick to inside of remaining paper. Continue to roll tightly to end of paper. Apply pressure to end for a minute until glue sets. Apply glue stick to wrong side of gold paper strip and roll on top of black paper, pressing end to set glue. Add wire, wrapping around paper a few times to begin. Add beads randomly as you wrap until you reach end of wire. Tuck end of wire under an adjacent piece to secure. Brush on Diamond Glaze to seal bead. Add a second or third coat to enhance shine. Let dry completely before sliding bead off skewer. Put a drop of Diamond Glaze on end of painted skewer before sliding bead onto top to help adhere.

Preparing the cover:
Lay black cardstock wrong side up in front of you. Make score lines according to measurements in diagram (A).

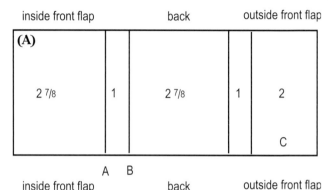

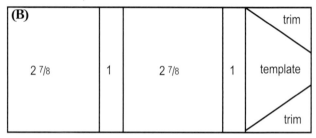

Trim Template:
Trim cover spine template on page 21 so it measures 3" x 5". Score vertical lines on either side of slots. Trim slots carefully with a sharp craft knife. Fold template on score lines.
On black cover stock, fold the first two score lines from the left marked A and B on diagram (A). Spine template should nest precisely into folds made in cover stock. Paper clip template into place. Mark a T at top of template and also at top of cover in pencil. Trace the four slots from template onto cover.
Remove template and cut slots from cover with a sharp craft knife. The slots should almost reach both folds, but not quite.

Hole punching Template:
Mark a T in the top right corner of a 3" x 5" ivory cardstock and fold in half lengthwise to make a 1 1/2" x 5" template for punching holes in signatures. Lay fold on spine over slots and mark a dot on the fold at the center of each slot. Match Ts on the cover and template before marking holes. Set cover and template aside. Hole-punching template should look something like diagram (C).

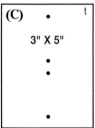

➤●━━ Cover Flap
       Template

Cover Flap:
Trim cover flap template. (Reserve for use later.) Punch a 1/8" hole where marking indicates. Lay on inside of far right panel of cover, marked C in (A), with narrow side of template facing out. See (B).
Trace right edges of template onto cardstock and punch hole where indicated. Trim where indicated in (B). Fold four score lines on cover to form a box shape, with right (trimmed) flap over left and trace the 1/8" hole onto left flap. Punch 1/8" hole in left flap. In addition, punch 1/8" hole in one of the triangles trimmed from flap. This will be used to prepare loop closure, so estimate center of triangle. It will be used for spacing only and then discarded. Cut a 1" long piece of 1/4" wide Wonder Tape in half to make two 1/2" pieces. Put a piece on inside to right and left of 1/8" hole in square flap of cover. See (D).
Don't remove protective cover on tape. On front side of same panel, lay scrap triangle over left flap and line up holes. Thread black cord through hole until a loop forms on front non-taped side. Slide painted skewer through loop. Triangle will act as a spacer to assure correct measurement of loop. Pull loop tightly against skewer. Carefully remove tape liner and expose adhesive on inside of cover. Press a loop end onto each side of tape. Trim any part of loop cord that extends beyond tape. Peel Xyron backing off black disc and stick disc over loop ends. Press with bone folder.
This should hide loop ends on inside of cover and secure ends further. Pull out skewer, discard triangle. If desired, enlarge right flap hole with 1/4" hole punch to thread loop more easily through.

A lovely handmade pin made from a glazed paper bead and a skewer holds this book closed. Remove it to reveal the treasures within.

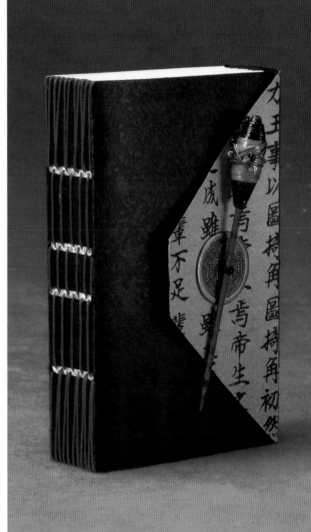

Asian Serenity Book

SIZE: 3" x 5"

MATERIALS:
1 piece heavy black cardstock 5" x 9 3/4"
66 sheets text paper 5" x 5 1/2"
Ivory cardstock for hole punching template 3" x 5"
1 cover flap template
1 cover spine template
1 piece Asian tissue
8 feet red waxed linen thread
1 Asian coin
4 paper clips
2 skewers
2 strips decorative paper
1 piece red decorative wire 8"
Various red, black and gold seed beads
1 black cover stock disc
1 piece black cord 2"

SUPPLIES:
Craft knife • Cutting mat • Metal ruler • Scissors • Bone folder • Awl
• Binder's needle • Glue stick • Red acrylic paint • Gem-Tac or Quick Grab
• Diamond Glaze • Wonder Tape • Asian writing stamp • Black Fabrico or
Brilliance Ink

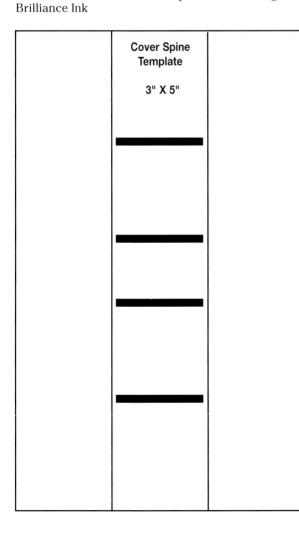

Cover Spine Template

3" X 5"

Continued from page 20.

6. Insert skewer in loop to secure closure.

Lay the Asian tissue right side down on your work table. Lay cover flap template right side up on top of tissue. Trace outside edge of template with a pencil and cut out. Apply a glue stick to wrong side of tissue and adhere the tissue to the right front flap of the cover. Re-punch 1/4" hole. Using dimensional glue such as Gem-Tac, adhere Asian coin to top of tissue, centered over 1/4" hole. Set the cover aside and let dry completely while you prepare signatures.

Preparing signatures:

Fold 66 sheets of text paper in half to make sheets 5" x 2³/4". Nest in groups of 6 to make 11 signatures. Mark each signature with a T in top right corner. Using the hole punching template made previously, nest template inside first signature, matching Ts, and punch four holes according to template. Repeat for remaining ten signatures.

Sewing book:

Book will be bound from back to front, or from 11th signature to 1st. Thread a needle with red waxed linen thread. Refer to (F), which shows stations as referenced in sewing directions. Notice head of book is at left, tail at right. Insert 11th signature into cover, matching Ts of cover and signature. Begin with needle on outside of 4th station.

Enter spine and signature, leaving 6" tail. Wrap thread tail around tail of book and signature and tie a square knot on inside of signature between 4th station and tail of book (G). Clip tail to 1/4". (*) Proceed to head of book with a running stitch: exit signature at 3rd station, re-enter at 2nd station and exit at 1st station.

Wrap thread over head of book and re-enter 11th signature at 1st station. Add 10th signature on top of 11th.

Wrap thread over head of book again and exit 10th signature at 1st station. Proceed to tail of book with a running stitch: enter 10th signature at 2nd station, exit at 3rd station. Enter at 4th station. Add 9th signature on top of 10th.

Wrap thread around tail of book and 10th signature, and enter 9th signature at 4th station. Wrap thread around tail again and re-enter 9th signature at 4th station. (#)

Note: this is different than the way thread was wrapped at head of book.

At head of book, wrap and re-enter signature before adding a new one. At tail of book, wrap after adding new signature, wrap again and re-enter same signature.

Repeat from (*) to (#), adding signatures where instructed until exiting 1st signature at 1st station. Wrap thread around head of book and tie a half hitch knot on inside to finish stitching. A half hitch knot is done by slipping needle under thread coming out of 1st station on inside of 1st signature. Pull thread until loop forms.

Slip needle through that loop and pull until knot forms. If desired, repeat this step to make a double half hitch knot for security. Clip thread to 1/4". When finished, spine of book should look like (H).

Close book, right flap over left. Bring closure loop up through coin with tip of beaded skewer and thread skewer through loop to secure.

E. bottom front flap

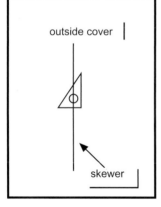

F. stations

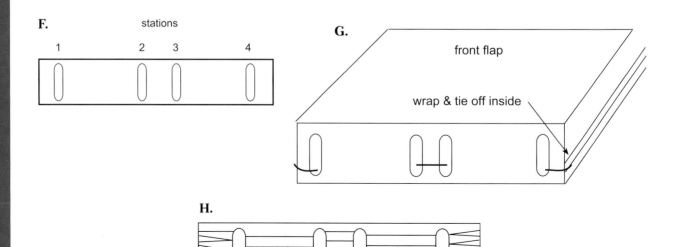

G. front flap

wrap & tie off inside

H.

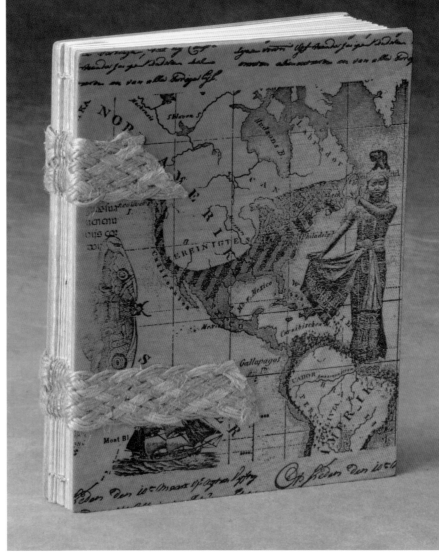

*W*oven tapes hold this book's wooden cover in place. Decorate with wood stain, inks and your favorite rubber stamp designs.

Sewing Over Tapes

SIZE: 6" x 8"
MATERIALS:
2 birchwood covers
    approximately 6" x 8"
Sandpaper: 1 piece 120 grit
    and 1 piece 220 grit
2 woven tapes 10" x 1"
32 sheets text paper 8 1/2" x 14"
2 pieces decorative end paper
    8" x 12"
1 piece decorative spine paper
    8" x 12"
3 yards waxed linen thread
2 pieces Tyvek 1/2" x 7"
1 hole punching jig 3" x 8"

SUPPLIES:
X-Acto knife and cutting mat or
Fiskars rotary trimmer • Awl • Glue
brush or sponge brayer • PVA glue
• Waxed paper • Wood stain •
Paintbrush • Binder's needle •
Bone folder • Stamps • Permanent
ink • Pencil

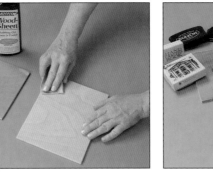 

1. Sand and stain birchwood covers. **2.** Stamp image with permanent ink.

INSTRUCTIONS:
Preparing the Covers:

Sand wood, starting with 120 grit sandpaper to smooth surface and rough edges of boards. Round edges and corners for softer appearance.

Use 220 grit sandpaper to ready wood for painting or staining. The smoother the surface is, the better your stamped images will look.

I used 2 coats of Minwax Wood Sheen, Manor Oak color, for a nice light stain that shows off the beauty of the natural wood.

Be sure to let it dry for several hours or overnight until the stickiness subsides.

I tried several types of pigment inks on the finished wood and nothing produced an image as sharp as Tsukineko's StazOn Ink. When stamping, keep in mind, the tapes will cover some of your image, so plan accordingly.

You may even prefer to finish sewing the text block before embellishing the covers to be certain of your art placement.

Continued on page 24.

Continued from page 23.

3. Sew signatures over woven tapes.

4. Fold end papers in half with right side together. Fold Tyvek strip in half and PVA glue to wrong side of fold of each end paper.

5. Glue the end papers to the book block.

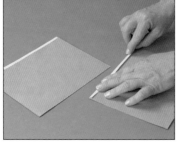

6. Trim woven tapes and glue to cover with PVA glue.

7. Attach covers to end paper with PVA glue.

Preparing text block:

Fold 32 sheets of 8¹/2" x 14" paper in half to 8¹/2" x 7". Use bone folder to make folds crisp. Nest four at a time to make 8 signatures. Label each signature in top right corner with pencil: T1, T2, T3 etc. to T8. • Since wood covers may vary, trim signatures to size. Trimming is most easily done with a Fiskars Rotary Trimmer. An X-Acto knife, ruler and cutting mat also work well. Trim height of signatures to 8". Measure width of book, subtract ¹/8" and cut open end of signatures to that width.

To prepare end papers and accordion fold spine piece, fold two decorative sheets in half with right sides together. Trim if necessary to match signatures. Set aside. • Trim other piece of decorative paper to same height as your signatures (around 8"). You will be making a 16 fold accordion piece. Fold the decorative paper in half to make a piece 6" x 8". Take each section and fold it in half again to make 4 folds. Don't worry about the direction of the folds yet. That will be adjusted at the end.

Now, take each new section of paper and fold in half again to make 8 folds. Then fold each of those 8 sections again to make 16 folds. Take your time and be precise about your folds as this piece will support the spine of your book. The result should look like this in profile, with the unprinted side facing up:

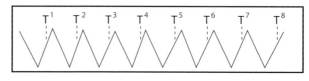

If it doesn't, just bend the folds in the opposite direction to match the drawing. Your 8 signatures will be nested inside these valley folds. With the accordion fold in front of you, unprinted side facing up, label each valley fold in pencil on the top right side from left to right: T1, T2, T3 etc. to match the signatures.

To prepare a punching pattern or jig, trim ivory cardstock to same height as signatures. Fold in half vertically to approximately 8" x 1¹/2" and lay it closed on work table with fold to the left. Make two pencil marks on fold, ¹/2" from top and bottom of jig. Make two more marks on fold, 1¹/2" from top and bottom of jig. Lay woven tapes across fold and make marks on fold at midpoint of each tape and on opposite sides of tapes. Make a T in top right corner of jig to indicate top.

This T will match up with Ts on signatures and valley folds of accordion spine piece when sewing holes are punched. Opened jig will have 8 holes and look something like this:

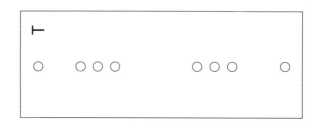

Prepare the signatures for sewing. Use a punching cradle, or simply punch holes in your usual manner. Punch holes in signatures and spine piece simultaneously, starting with signature marked T1 and nested in valley fold marked T1. Nest jig inside that and check that all Ts match in top right corner. Punch 8 holes according to pattern. Repeat with remaining 7 signatures, inserting each one in corresponding fold of spine piece before punching.

Sewing text block:

Thread needle with waxed linen. Fold one 10" woven tape in half to 1" x 5" and lightly draw a line in pencil at fold. Make another line ¹/2" from first. This is where you will position tape to attach it to spine. Repeat for other tape.

Nest eighth signature in eighth fold of accordion. Lay on work table with spine facing you, with head of book to your left and tail to your right. Book will be sewn from back to front, sewing accordion fold and signature as one piece. For ease of understanding, holes will be numbered 1 through 8 starting on right side as spine faces you.

Insert threaded needle into 1st hole and come out 3rd hole, skipping 2nd hole for now, leaving 3" tail. This will bring the needle out through center of tape. Insert needle through 2nd hole, wrapping thread over tape. The only place tape is pierced is at center. Exit signature at 4th hole and insert needle back in 3rd hole again, wrapping thread over tape. This simple wrapping pattern is repeated for other tape. Exit at 6th hole, splitting tape.

Wrap around tape and go into 5th hole. Come out 7th hole. Wrap tape and go back through 6th hole. Exit 8th hole to finish sewing eighth signature.

Pull thread snugly as you sew, pulling parallel to spine.

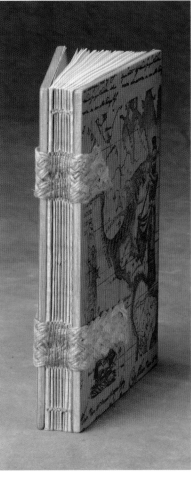

*S*hown *here are the book's inside text pages and a view of the spine of the bound book.*

Place signature marked T7 into accordion fold marked T7, with both marks on left side. Insert needle into 8th hole of seventh signature. Pull thread to snug two signatures together.

Follow same wrapping pattern as eighth signature, only in opposite direction. Exit 6th hole, splitting tape just above spot tape was split on previous signature. Wrap thread over tape and insert needle into 7th hole. Exit 5th hole, wrap the tape and go back into 6th hole. Exit 3rd hole, wrap tape and go into 4th hole. Exit 2nd hole, wrap tape and go back into 3rd hole. Exit 1st hole to complete sewing on seventh signature.

At the end of the seventh signature connect two signatures with a square knot using tail. Do not clip tail yet.

Repeat this sewing pattern, adding signatures. Even numbered signatures (8, 6, 4, 2) will be sewn from right to left in same pattern as eighth signature was sewn. Odd numbered signatures (7, 5, 3, 1) will be sewn from left to right in same pattern as seventh signature was sewn. • Add sixth signature. At end of signature, attach to seventh signature with kettle stitch.

Slip needle behind thread that connects seventh and eighth signatures, with tip of needle facing head of book. Pull needle through until a loop forms in thread. Slip needle through loop from right and pull snugly, forming a tight knot. This kettle stitch will be repeated at end of every signature before next signature is added. Do not use tail again to connect any signatures.

Add fifth signature, sewing from left to right, and connect fifth signature to sixth signature using kettle stitch. Add remaining signatures in same manner. Attach last signature to previous one with a double kettle stitch.

Trim sewing thread and tail to about 1/4". Tuck ends into accordion folds and secure each with PVA glue.

Attaching covers:

Fold each Tyvek piece in half vertically to 7" x 1/4". Using PVA glue, glue each Tyvek piece to wrong side of fold of each end paper. This will reinforce end paper fold to prevent wear and tear as book is opened and closed. Lay a sheet of waxed paper over one folded end paper, leaving about 1/2" exposed at fold. Apply PVA to that strip of paper. Remove waxed paper and lay end paper on text block with glued fold to the left, attaching end paper to text block and not accordion piece. Burnish strip with a wad of waxed paper or bone folder to secure. Repeat for other end paper.

With book in front of you, tapes to the left, you should be able to see the right (decorated) side of the little accordion piece. Slip a piece of scrap paper under the accordion piece and apply PVA to the right (decorated) side of this strip. Carefully lay front cover on top of this spine piece, checking that cover is aligned with all edges of text block. Secure strip by rubbing with a bone folder or wad of wax paper. Close cover and repeat to attach back cover. Allow glue to dry completely before proceeding.

Trim tapes to desired length and shape. If desired, alter color of tapes by stippling with permanent ink, masking spine as you stipple. When tapes are ready, apply PVA glue to inside of tape and attach to covers. Apply weight and allow glue to dry completely.

Apply PVA glue to wrong side of end paper adjacent to cover. Apply glue evenly and completely to all edges of paper. Press end paper to cover gently and evenly from spine edge out, smoothing as you go. Rub gently with a bone folder or wax paper to smooth. Insert a clean piece of scrap paper and close cover.

Repeat for the back cover.

Be certain that both end papers are smooth before weighting book and leaving to dry.

*Long Tall Sally stands a magnificent 11"
high, and is accented with a woven paper
cover and oodles of fibers.*

Long Tall Sally

by Sally Hill and M. K. Seckler

SIZE: 4¹/₂" x 11¹/₄"

MATERIALS:

2 pieces book board for covers 11¹/₄" x 4³/₈"
1 piece book board for spine 11¹/₄" x 2¹/₂"
1 piece decorative cover paper 13" x 13"
2 pieces end paper 11" x 4¹/₄"
1 piece spine cover paper 11" x 4"
1 piece Tyvek 23" x 4"
1 piece decorative paper for cover art 6¹/₂" x 4¹/₂"
5 strips decorative paper and 10 fibers for cover
11 pieces brown waxed linen thread 30" each
11 bundles decorative fibers
Small beads for spine decoration
6 sheets Echo text paper 8¹/₂" x 11"
6 sheets Royal Fiber Kraft text paper 8¹/₂" x 11"
6 sheets olive text paper 8¹/₂" x 11"
5 sheets Astroparche Sand text paper 8¹/₂" x 11"
5 sheets Royal Fiber Balsa text paper 8¹/₂" x 11"
5 sheets Royal Fiber Spice text paper 8¹/₂" x 11"
11 each A2 Kraft envelopes
1 bead threader

SUPPLIES:

Craft knife • Cutting mat • Scissors • Bone folder • Awl •
Dremel or hand drill with ¹/₁₆" bit • PVA glue • Newsprint or
glue paper • ¹/₁₆" hole punch • Waxed paper • Temporary
bond tape or glue stick • Binder's needle with small eye •
Davey board cradle • ³/₁₆" square dowel

Preparing cover: Measure 5" from bottom of Tyvek strip
and draw a line across strip in pencil. Measure ⁵/₈" from left
side above line and draw a line up strip about 6". Apply PVA
glue sparingly to spine board (11¹/₄" x 2¹/₂"), and let dry a
few seconds, just until sheen leaves glue. Apply board to
place on Tyvek just above and to the right of lines you drew,
so board is positioned in center of strip. Lay ³/₁₆" wide
square dowel next to spine board as a spacer. Apply PVA glue
to strip left of spine board and place one cover board right
next to dowel. Be sure bottom of cover board is even with
bottom of spine board. Remove dowel before it adheres to
Tyvek. Repeat procedure for right cover board. Flip cover
boards over carefully and burnish Tyvek using a wad of
waxed paper. Turn cover boards over again. Apply PVA glue
to top of Tyvek strip and fold over onto spine and cover
boards. Repeat with bottom strip. Burnish with waxed paper,
leaving grooves in spaces between cover boards and spine.

Lay cover paper (13" x 13") wrong side up on glue paper
covered work surface. Measure ³/₄" from bottom and draw a
horizontal line on cover paper with a pencil. Measure ⁵/₈"
from left side of cover paper and draw a vertical line with a
pencil. To avoid wrinkling of cover paper, apply glue sparingly to one portion of cover at a time and allow to dry slightly before applying board to cover paper. Work with a damp
brush to thin glue and help brush move more smoothly.
Keep water nearby to dampen brush occasionally.

Don't overdo the water! Begin with left cover. Apply
glue, let dry slightly, then apply board to cover paper in corner where two pencil lines meet. Turn over and burnish with
waxed paper. Apply glue to spine board and repeat burnishing. Apply glue to back cover and burnish again. Miter corners of remaining cover paper with scissors, leaving about
¹/₈" extra at corner to accommodate height of board.

Apply PVA glue sparingly to strip to left of front cover
and fold over edge of board. Press with waxed paper to
secure. Repeat for right side, top and bottom. Apply PVA glue

to spine cover paper (11" x 4"). Work quickly to minimize curling.
Apply spine cover paper centered over spine area and burnish with
waxed paper. Repeat for two end papers, centering each over cover
before applying glue to check for placement. Burnish to adhere.

Preparing spine for sewing: Trim templates with scissors or craft
knife. Each should measure 8¹/₂" tall x 2¹/₂" wide. Score solid vertical
lines on two signature hole punching templates and set aside. Apply
temporary bond such as Hermafix or glue stick to back of spine hole
punching template. Apply template to inside of spine centered from
top to bottom. Using a sharp awl, mark all 50 holes on spine.

Press down with awl to create solid holes for drilling. Remove
template and set aside. If any residue from temporary bond remains,
rub off. Using ¹/₁₆" bit, drill holes through spine to make sewing easier.

Preparing signatures: There are two different templates for signature hole punching. Odd numbered signatures will have a different set
of holes than even numbered signatures. Horizontal lines at top and
bottom of each template will be used to center envelopes for punching. Fold each of three different types of text paper in half to form
sheets 11" x 4¹/₄". Nest in groups of three sheets, one of each type.
Kraft envelopes will be nested in each signature. Mark each signature
in top right corner: T1, T3, T5, etc. to indicate top. These are odd signatures. Fold odd # signature hole punching template along
center score line and nest inside first signature with Ts matching. Punch five
holes in signature. Repeat for remaining five signatures. Mark
envelopes with T in top right corner by flap. Lay side of first envelope
without flap next to fold of template, centered between two lines.

Be sure T on envelope matches T on signature. Using ¹/₁₆" hole
punch, make five half-holes along edge of envelope, just nicking edge
to create holes for sewing. Repeat with five envelopes to make a total
of six, one for each signature. Nest one envelope inside each signature
with holes in fold of signature. Envelope holes should line up with signature holes. Set signatures aside along with template to avoid confu-
sion later. • Fold remaining text paper and nest in groups of three, one
of each type, to make five signatures. Mark signatures T2, T4, T6 etc. in
top right corner. Fold even # signature hole punching template along
center score line and nest inside first signature with Ts matching.
Punch four holes in signature. Repeat for other four signatures, and
with remaining five envelopes according to previous directions.

Don't forget to mark envelopes with a T, and match Ts when
punching holes. Each envelope will be nested inside a signature.
Arrange signatures in order: T1, T2, T3 etc.

1. Prepare cover assembly.
Use a ³/₁₆" dowel as a spacer
to create gutter without
measuring.

2. Prepare spine for
sewing. Mark holes with
an awl according to tem-
plate. Drill with ¹/₁₆" bit.

3. Prepare the odd numbered
signatures and envelopes.
Mark and punch them
according to the template.

4. Prepare even numbered
signatures and envelopes.
Mark and punch them
according to the template.

Continued on page 28.

Continued from page 27.

5. Sew the signatures and envelopes.

6. Add beads according to spine template pattern.

7. Attach fibers to spine with square knot.

8. Create a weave for the cover using paper and fibers. Attach to the cover with PVA glue.

Sewing book:

Book is sewn with a simple long stitch. It is complicated by the fact that you will be sewing through envelopes and beading the spine. If you are a beginner, you may wish to omit these two steps and simply sew signatures without envelopes or beads.

Looking at the spine from the outside of the book, and counting from left to right, beaded signatures will be numbers 4, 6, and 8. Notice pattern of holes on spine. Odd numbered columns have five holes and even numbered columns have four. If you have punched your signatures correctly, all holes should correspond to holes in appropriate column on spine.

Thread needle with brown waxed linen thread. You will be sewing signatures into first column of holes on spine, working from back to front. Refer to spine hole-punching guide at column marked 1. Starting at top of book on outside, enter spine and leave a 6" tail. Enter top hole of signature and then top hole of envelope.

Be careful when pulling thread through; pull straight to avoid tearing envelope or signature. Now, exit envelope, sig-

samples created by April Mott and M. K. Seckler

nature and spine at 2nd hole down column. Be careful to stay in same column. Re-enter spine at 3rd hole down column, going through signature and envelope. Exit spine at 4th hole. Re-enter spine at 5th hole of column, going through all layers. Reverse direction and come back up to top of signature one hole at a time.

When you finish by exiting spine at 2nd hole, tie off thread with square knot using 6" tail. Do not cut off threads, as you will use these to tie fibers onto spine after sewing is complete. Remove needle, thread with another piece of waxed linen and sew next signature using the same long stitch.

Note: 2nd signature only has 4 holes and that beginning hole is lower than beginning hole of 1st signature. Sew 2nd and 3rd signatures using long stitch described above.

When sewing 4th signature, add 17 beads between 2nd and 3rd holes on spine. Begin at 1st hole, enter spine and exit at 2nd hole. Thread 17 beads onto thread and enter 3rd hole, exit at 4th hole, go back up to 3rd hole, exit at 2nd hole and tie off with square knot at 1st hole.

Sew 5th signature without beads using the long stitch. Sew 6th signature down spine using the long stitch, but when exiting 4th hole, add 17 beads on thread, come back up and re-enter 3rd hole. Exit at 2nd hole, add 17 more beads and tie off with square knot at 1st hole. Sew 7th signature without beads, using long stitch. Sew 8th signature the same way as 4th signature, adding beads between 2nd and 3rd holes on spine. Remaining three signatures will be sewn without beads, using same long stitch.

Separate fibers to make 11 bundles with one strand of each fiber. Tie one bundle to top of each signature with square knot at midpoint of each bundle using waxed linen thread. Leave waxed linen thread to blend into each bundle or cut remainder off after tying a sturdy knot.

Preparing cover art:

Use base piece of paper cut evenly or tear one or both long sides to make rough edges. Leave top and bottom edge straight so piece remains $6\frac{1}{2}$" tall. Finished piece should be $6\frac{1}{2}$" tall and $3\frac{3}{4}$" wide when finished tearing or trimming. Lay face down, oriented vertically on cutting mat. Draw 12 horizontal lines, $\frac{1}{2}$" apart with a pencil.

Make a vertical line about $\frac{1}{2}$" from left side and do the same on right side. Vertical lines will be starting and stopping guides when cutting horizontal lines for weave. Cut lines straight or wavy, as desired.

Turn paper back to right side and weave 5 strips through cuts. If desired, tear ends of strips after weaving is complete to give a more interesting finish. After paper is woven, weave fibers, 2 at a time, over each paper strip using the bead-threader.

Be sure to hold onto paper while pulling threads.

When art piece is finished, apply PVA glue to wrong side and adhere to front of book.

Glue down fibers coming from top of weave so they don't hang.

Templates are on pages 30 and 31.

Continued from page 29.

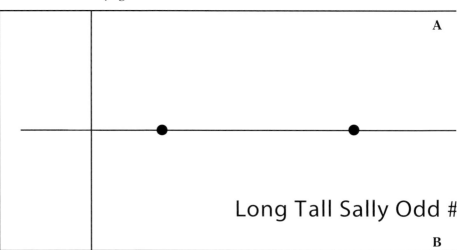

A

Long Tall Sally Odd #

B

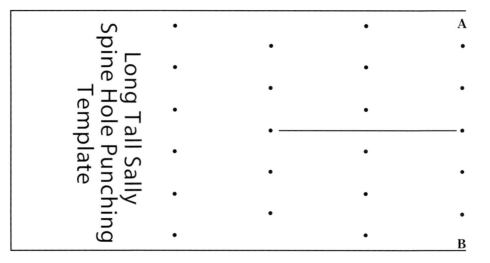

A

Long Tall Sally
Spine Hole Punching
Template

B

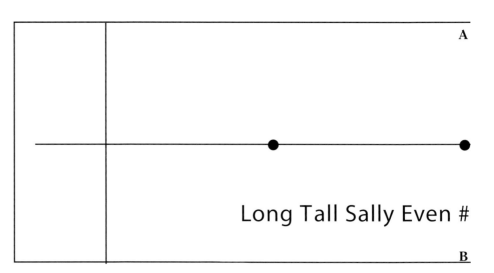

A

Long Tall Sally Even #

B

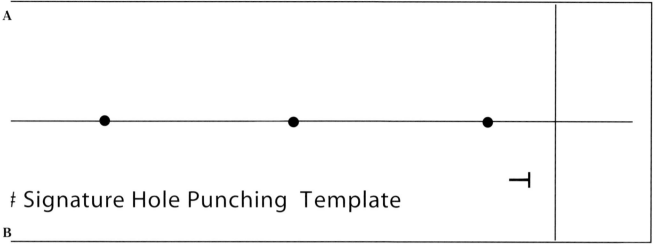

ƭ Signature Hole Punching Template

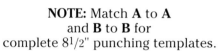

NOTE: Match **A** to **A**
and **B** to **B** for
complete 8¹/₂" punching templates.

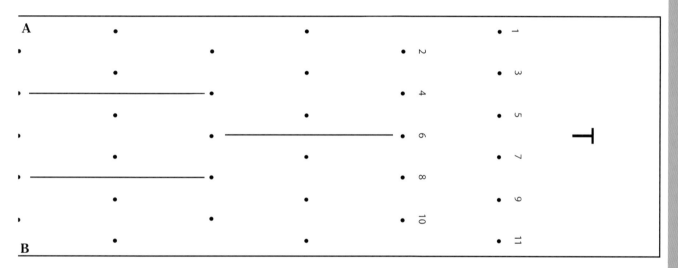

NOTE: Match **A** to **A**
and **B** to **B** for
complete 8¹/₂" punching templates.

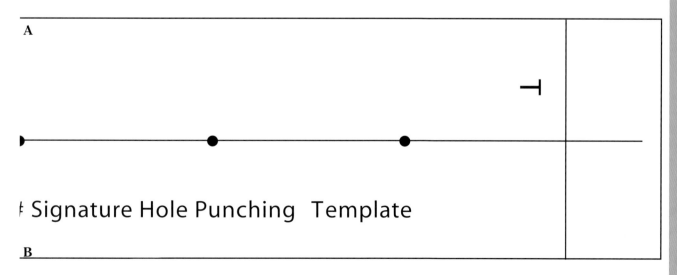

ƭ Signature Hole Punching Template

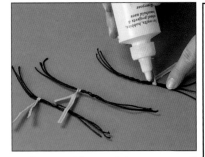

1. Group 12 cord linen into 3 bundles. Tie with twist tie and glue in center.

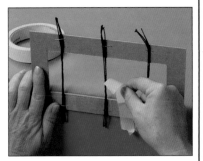

2. Cut a 1" book board frame.

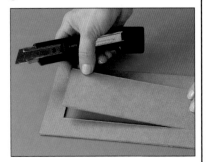

3. Staple the bundles to marks on the frame.

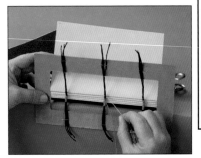

4. Sew signatures around wrapped cords.

5. Prepare covers. Using hole punching template to make nine holes in each cover. Set the eyelets.
Continued on page 34.

T
Raven's Foot Binding

Cover Template

SIZE: 4 /2" x 71/4"
MATERIALS:
2 pieces book board 41/2" x 71/4"
2 pieces cover paper 91/4" x 61/2"
2 pieces end paper 7" x 81/2"
32 pieces text paper 7" x 81/2"
1 piece book board 9" x 41/2"
3 twist ties
9 pieces 12 ply black waxed linen cord, 6"
1 piece 7 ply butterscotch waxed linen
    thread, 2 yards
1 page antique French text for
    cover decoration
1 piece black core matboard 25/8" x 11/8"
18 each 1/8" gold long reach eyelets
1 cover hole punching template
1 signature hole punching template

SUPPLIES:
2 small binder clips • Craft knife • Cutting board • Metal-edged ruler • Awl • Bone folder • Scissors • Binder's needle • Glue stick • PVA glue • Glue brush • Masking tape • 1/8" eyelet setter • Hammer • Dremel drill with 1/8" bit or heavy-duty 1/8" hole punch • Small decorative stamp • Gold embossing powder • Gold ink • Varitone Ink or Topaz Cat's Eye • Gold *Krylon* leafing pen • Waxed paper • Scrap paper

Preparing wrapped cords:

Separate 9 pieces of black waxed linen cord into three groups of three threads each. Put a drop of PVA glue at midpoint of each bundle. Wrap a twist tie around each bundle to hold together while glue dries.

Making sewing frame:

Using piece of book board measuring 9" x 4 /2", mark 1" in from each corner. With craft knife, connect these four marks to create a 1" wide frame, measuring 7" x 21/2" inside. Discard center piece of book board.

Preparing signatures:

Fold 32 pieces of text paper in half to 7" x 41/4". Nest sheets in eight signatures of four sheets each. Mark a T in top right corner of each signature. Fold two end papers in half, right sides together, and wrap around first and last signatures. Trim signature hole punching template, score center line and fold on line with markings of template together. Nest template in the middle of first signature with Ts matching.

Punch three holes according to template using awl and Davey Board cradle (if you have one). Repeat for remaining 7 signatures.

Preparing covers:

Cover first piece of book board with cover paper as follows: Lay a piece of cover paper face down on work surface. Apply glue stick to entire piece of book board. Center on piece of cover paper. Miter all four corners, leaving an amount in each corner equal to height of book board – about 1/8". Apply glue stick to remaining flaps, one at a time, and wrap around board. Smooth cover paper with a wad of waxed paper to insure good adhesion. Repeat for other cover.

Trim cover hole-punching template. Mark each cover with a T on the inside to signify the top. Lay template over outside of first cover, matching Ts of template and cover.

Mark holes with awl. Drill nine holes using a 1/8" Dremel bit or Japanese screw punch. Set long reach eyelets in holes with setter and hammer. Lay template on inside of back cover board with Ts matching. Repeat from * for the back cover. Set covers aside.

Signature Template

T

The Raven's Foot binding wraps around the cover, threading through eyelets. This provides an interesting decorative accent while holding the book together securely. The embellishments are a piece of French text and a piece of black matboard embossed and edged in gold leaf.

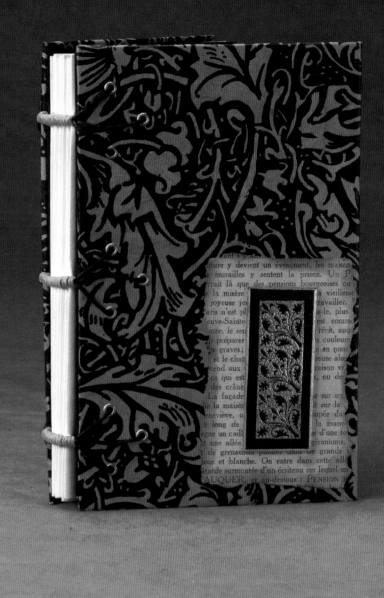

You may choose to add black matboard between several signatures as dividers for special sections. Photo mounts and pockets are an excellent way to brighten your pages as you tell your story.

Continued from page 32.

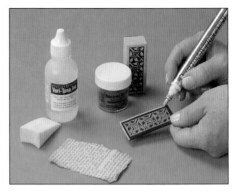

6. Attach the covers by threading cords over outside of cover and through eyelets.

7. Glue cords down with PVA glue. Hammer flat. Attach end paper with PVA glue.

8. Prepare cover art. Dab French text with Varitone ink and heat. Emboss black matboard and edge with gold leaf pen.

Sewing book:

Mark sewing frame with a T at one end to signify the top. Lay frame horizontally in front of you with T to your left. Lay one signature next to the frame horizontally with Ts matching. Draw three vertical lines in pencil on frame that correspond with holes punched in the signature. Remove twist ties from cord bundles. Staple first bundle so cords are taut, centered on first line, top and bottom. Repeat for the other two bundles. With masking tape, tape frame to the edge of the work table with thread bundles facing you and T to your left. Stack signatures with Ts to your left in order, with a wrapped signature on top and bottom of the stack. This will be the order of sewing: from 8th signature to 1st.

Thread needle with butterscotch waxed linen thread. Holes will be numbered 1 to 3 from head to tail. Lay 8th and 7th signatures on table with folds nestled next to cords, with T of signatures matching T of frame. The wrapped or 8th signature will be on table and 7th will be stacked on top. Start sewing slightly below glued place on cords. If necessary, put a book on table before stacking signatures for proper spacing. The same length of black cords should remain at front of book as at back, to ensure there is enough cord to attach both covers. Sewing will begin inside 7th signature, in first hole at left bundle of cords.

Insert needle from inside and pull thread through, leaving a 4" tail. Thread should exit to right of cords. Tape tail to left side of frame to secure until you tie it off.

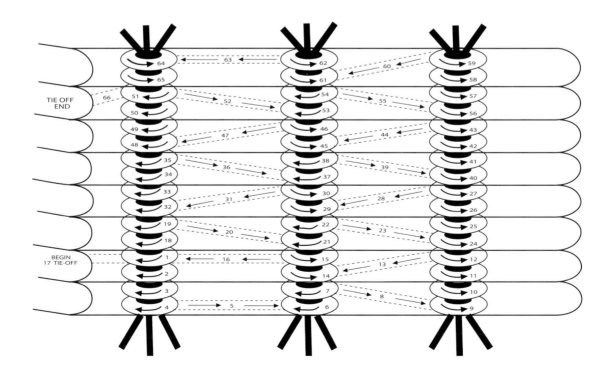

Refer to diagram as you sew. Wrap sewing thread around first bundle of cords four times according to drawing, wrapping in a clockwise direction, or right to left. Enter 8th signature at first hole, exit 8th signature at 2nd hole, to right of cords. Take your time wrapping cords neatly, not overlapping or twisting threads. Wraps should be snug so no black thread shows between butterscotch wraps.

Wrap cords twice in a clockwise direction, according to drawing, and re-enter 8th signature at second hole. Exit 8th signature at 3rd hole, this time to left of cords and wrap cords four times in a counterclockwise direction. Enter 7th signature at third hole. Clip the two signatures at head and tail with binder clips to help keep them aligned while sewing. Exit 7th signature at second hole to left of cords, wrap cords twice in a counterclockwise direction and re-enter 7th signature at second hole. Untape tail and tie off at first hole with a square knot. Trim off tail to 1/4". Exit 7th signature at first hole to right of cords. Add 6th signature and adjust binder clips to accommodate it. Wrap cords twice in a clockwise direction, re-enter 6th signature at first hole and exit at second hole to right of cords. Wrap twice in a clockwise direction, re-enter 6th signature at second hole and exit at first hole to left of cords. Wrap four times in a counterclockwise direction. Add 5th signature and adjust binder clips. Continue with sewing until you are ready to tie-off.

Normally at head of book you would exit to right of cords and wrap in a counterclockwise direction. For tie-off, exit 1st signature at first hole to right of cords. Wrap twice according to drawing and re-enter 2nd signature at first hole. Tie off with a double half hitch knot. To do this, slip needle under thread connecting first and second stations.

Pull thread until loop forms. Slip needle through loop and pull snugly. Repeat to form a double half hitch. Trim thread to 1/4".

Attaching covers:

Remove cords from frame with staple remover. Lay front cover over front of book, matching T of cover with T on signatures. Separate threads of each bundle and thread each one through an eyelet from outside cover to inside.

When all threads are through eyelets, dot PVA glue on inside of cover and press cords into glue one at a time. Leave a gap between book block and cover equal to thickness of cover board, or cords will be too tight for book to open and close properly. When all cords are glued onto cover, test tension by closing cover. Adjust if necessary. When tension is correct, trim each cord to 1" to make an even line on cover. Add a bit more glue to secure. If desired, hammer cords flat after glue dries and before gluing end paper to cover. When front cover is complete, lay a sheet of waxed paper between cover and end paper and repeat procedure with back cover.

Gluing end papers:

Slide a piece of scrap paper between end paper and first page of text block. Apply PVA glue to end paper up to 1/8" of spine. Remove scrap paper and close cover. Be sure position of end paper is correct before smoothing onto cover with a wad of waxed paper. Repeat for back cover.

Adding cover art:

Emboss a small stamp in gold onto black core matboard. Edge board with Gold Krylon leafing pen. Tear French text to make a mat for embossed art. Age torn edges with Topaz Cat's Eye or Varitone Ink. Attach French text with glue stick to lower right hand corner of front cover.

Attach matboard piece centered on text with PVA glue.

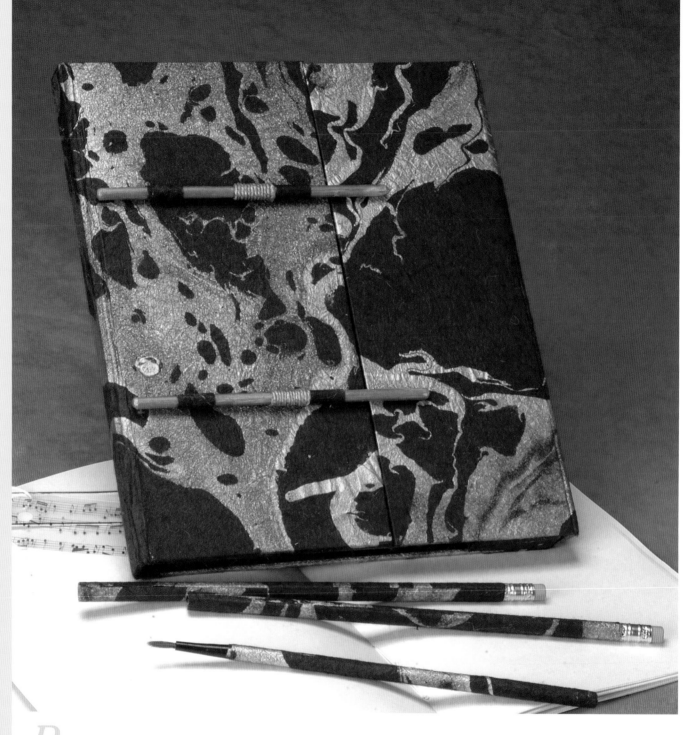

*B*eautiful marbled paper covers this Asian flavor
art book with gold bamboo skewers as closures.
Open the covers to see the special hideaway.

Geisha's Hideaway Spine Hole Punching Template

COVER MATERIALS:
1 cover template
2 pieces book board 7" x 8⁵/8"
1 piece book board 4" x 8⁵/8"
1 piece book board 3" x 8⁵/8"
2 pieces book board ¹/2" x 8⁵/8"
1 piece cover paper 18" x 10⁵/8"" (blue marble)
1 piece cover paper 9" x 10⁵/8" (black Tanabata)
1 piece cover paper 3¹/2" x 8¹/2" (black Tanabata)
1 piece cover paper 5" x 8¹/2" (black Tanabata))
2 pieces cover paper 7" x 8¹/2" (black Tanabata)

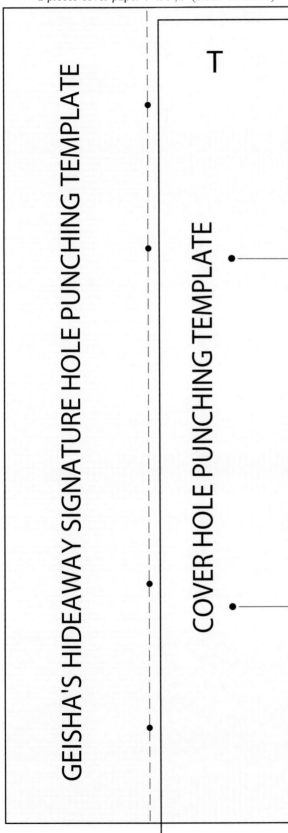

GEISHA'S HIDEAWAY SIGNATURE HOLE PUNCHING TEMPLATE

COVER HOLE PUNCHING TEMPLATE

T

Geisha's Hideaway

SIZE: 7¹/4" x 8⁵/8"
SUPPLIES: Metal ruler • Bone folder • Craft knife • Cutting mat • PVA glue • Glue brush • Awl • Glue stick • Binding needle • Square dowels (2 each ³/16" and ¹/4") • Davey board cradle (optional) • Waxed paper

Making the Cover:

Trim cover hole-punching template. Lay on top of an 8⁵/8" x 4" book board. Mark a T at top of board in pencil. Mark 8 holes with an awl.

T

Be sure each hole is at least ¹/16" so slits are wide enough to accommodate closure strips. Connect each pair of holes horizontally using craft knife, making 4 slits each measuring about ³/4" long and ¹/16" wide. • Lay 18" x 10⁵/8" decorative cover paper face down horizontally. Measure 1" from bottom and draw a line parallel to edge with a pencil.

Measure 1" from left edge and draw a line parallel to edge. Position first piece of cover board with T facing paper, and bottom corner sitting where two lines meet. Lay out cover pieces in the following order, using dowels as spacers to avoid measuring and marking gutters: Add a ¹/4" spacer on right side of cover board. Place a ¹/2" x 8⁵/8" spine piece next to spacer. Place a ³/16" spacer next to spine piece. Place one 7" x 8¹/2" board next to the spacer. Lay a ³/16" spacer, then add the other ¹/2" spine, followed by a ¹/4" spacer. Add 3" x 8⁵/8" board last.

There should be a 1" border around the layout. All bottom edges of boards should be on the line drawn parallel to the bottom edge of the paper. • Beginning with the left side, apply glue stick or PVA glue to each board and apply each to cover paper, removing spacers as you go, burnishing well. Gently burnish gutters formed by spacers.

When all five pieces of board are glued to cover paper, miter four corners, leaving an amount of paper in each corner equal to height of board. Before gluing flaps over sides of boards, mark position of slits on front cover and cut cover paper to match slits. Use awl to press paper into slits so you have clean gaps. When gluing and folding left flap over, recut slits on that side. Glue right flap, then top and bottom flaps, gently burnishing gutters. • Cover remaining 7" x 8⁵/8" board with 9" x 10⁵/8" cover paper, mitering corners and gluing flaps. Set aside while preparing closure.

1. Using cover hole punching template, mark the holes in book board. Cut 4 slits in the cover.

2. Lay out boards in order, allowing proper spaces. Glue cover paper using glue stick or PVA.

3. Score strips. Fold over and glue in place.

4. Mark each closure skewer. Apply PVA glue and wrap gold-painted hemp around skewer within marks.

5. Thread strips through slits. Slide skewers through strips until twine is between strips. Glue strip ends with PVA.

Continued on page 38.

Continued from page 37.

6. Complete front cover by gluing last covered board to closure piece at first gutter.

7. Adhere end papers to cover with PVA glue. Add flaps that hold tacket binding.

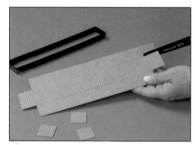

8. Construct the pencil box frame.

9. Cover pencil box frame with handmade paper.

CLOSURE MATERIALS:
2 gold bamboo skewers 5"
2 pieces gold hemp twine 11"
4 pieces cover paper 1¹/₂" x 4" (black Tanabata)

Making closure:

Take 4 strips measuring 1¹/₂" x 4". Score each one as follows on 4" side: ³/₈" from one side, ¹/₂" from other side. Using a glue stick, glue folds over to make four reinforced strips. When sides are folded wrong sides together and glued, strip measures ⁵/₈" wide.

Mark gold painted skewers 2¹/₄" from left end and 2" from right end. Cut gold twine in half. Apply PVA glue to ³/₄" space in center of skewer and wrap twine around to make a stopper. Cut ends of twine at an angle to help adhere to skewer. Cut off any excess twine. Press twine onto skewer until glue starts to set. Repeat for other skewer. Let dry completely.

Thread one strip, seamed side toward cover, through one of the slits in cover, so ends are on inside of cover and a loop is on outside of cover. Repeat for other three strips. Thread one skewer through top set of loops so side of the skewer that has 2¹/₄" of wood showing is on left side. When twine section is between loops, tighten ends of loops from back so paper loops are snug against skewer.

Repeat for other skewer. Note that if you reverse the direction that the skewer goes into the loops, the closure will not work properly. When each skewer slides as far to the right as it will go, it clears left edge of book and extends over seam to lock cover closed. When each skewer slides as far to the left as it can go, it should just clear the seam, allowing right flap to be lifted. Test this before gluing strips on back of cover. If it doesn't work, reverse direction of skewers. When closure is working properly, glue strips to inside cover using PVA glue. Glue ends in opposite directions so none overlap.

Gluing end papers: Apply PVA glue to the wrong side of 5" x 8¹/₂" decorative cover paper. Apply this piece to inside of cover assembly at right edge, covering right flap, right spine and about 1" beyond spine. Apply PVA glue to wrong side of 3¹/₂" x 8¹/₂" decorative cover paper, and apply this piece centered over left spine piece. Burnish both pieces with a wad of waxed paper, taking care to gently burnish gutters.

Apply PVA glue to entire back side of closure flap. Apply 7" x 8⁵/₈" piece covered earlier to glued area as follows: covered side facing glued area with left edges lining up as you look at closure. If done properly, right side will protrude beyond closure flap by 3". When two pieces are firmly glued together, find two decorative cover papers measuring 7" x 8¹/₂". Score one ¹/₄", apply glue stick to ¹/₄" area and fold over with wrong sides together so paper now measures 6³/₄" x 8¹/₂". Repeat for other paper.

Apply a thin line of PVA glue to 3 unfolded edges of one piece and glue into place on the left side of book block with folded edge toward first gutter. Do the same for other piece, but apply with folded side just beyond second gutter. Cover assembly is complete.

BOOK BLOCK MATERIALS:
32 sheets text paper 8¹/₂" x 11"
1¹/₂ yards white waxed linen thread
1 piece heavy black cardstock 7¹/₂" x 4¹/₂"
1 piece Tyvek 7¹/₂" x 1"
1 signature hole punching jig
1 spine hole punching jig

Making book block: Fold 32 sheets of text paper in half to 8¹/₂" x 5¹/₂". Nest in four signatures of eight sheets each. Mark each signature in top right corner with a T. Trim signature hole-punching template and score on dotted line. Nest template inside first signature, making sure Ts match, and punch holes according to template. Repeat remaining three signatures. Score heavy black cardstock lengthwise at 2" and 2¹/₂" from left side. Apply glue stick to one side of the Tyvek and apply the Tyvek centered over those score lines. Burnish well to assure a good bond and then fold along the score lines.

Mark top of Tyvek with a T. Trim spine hole-punching template and score along dashed lines.
Fold on score lines. Nest template inside heavy black cardstock, making sure Ts match.
Punch 16 holes in cardstock according to template.

Sewing signatures: Nest first signature in fold of cardstock. Signature will be sewn into first vertical row of holes. Insert needle into inside top hole of signature. Pull thread through leaving 2" tail, and exit top hole of cardstock. Enter 2nd hole of spine and signature. Tie off with tail in a square knot. Snip thread and tail at ¹/₄". Repeat for bottom set of holes. Repeat with remaining three signatures.

To insert book block into cover, fold wings back in opposite direction, away from book block. Fold cover backwards and insert wings into two sections of end paper with folded edges. Slide into place as cover is closed.

10. Adhere pencil box to right side of base.

11. Score stiff cardstock. Adhere Tyvek strip over score lines with PVA glue.

12. Nest spine hole punching template in tacket binding spine and punch holes using the awl.

13. Sew prepared signatures into tacket binding with waxed linen thread.

*S*lide open the clasps of this magical book to find a box holding pencils and brushes hidden within.

PENCIL BOX MATERIALS:
2 pieces black mat board $1/2$" x $81/2$"
2 pieces black mat board $1/2$" x $11/4$"
1 piece chipboard $11/4$" x 11"
1 piece cover paper 4" x 11" (black Tanabata)
3 pieces cover paper 1" x $63/4$" (blue marble)
2 pencils, 1 paintbrush

Making pencil box:

Tape black matboard strips together with $1/2$" Red Liner tape to form a box frame. Center box frame on chipboard. Mark four outside corners with pencil dots on chipboard. Connect dots with dashed lines.

Measure 1" beyond each side and draw another solid line box around dashed line box. It should measure about $101/2$" x $35/8$" Cut out chipboard on solid line. Cut a 1" square from each corner. This is the pattern you will trace on wrong side of 4" x 11" cover paper. Cut out. and score on dashed lines. Lay paper wrong side up and apply glue stick to four flaps.

Drop box frame onto paper so box fits inside score lines. Wrap four flaps up and over frame one at a time. Burnish with a bone folder to assure a good bond. Apply PVA glue lightly to bottom of box and align box inside cover assembly next to book block.

Double-check that box will fit before applying glue to bottom.

This assembly is a close fit so if book block is tight against pencil box, remove and trim telescoping of pages to fit. Trim each signature individually with a heavy duty craft knife or rotary trimmer.

Covering the pencils and paintbrush:

Apply glue stick to wrong side of a remaining piece of cover paper paper and wrap around a pencil. Trim as necessary. Repeat for other two items.

Drop utensils in the pencil box.

14. Insert the book block into the cover.

15. Cover pencils and paintbrush with cover paper using glue stick.

*P*iano hinge books are assembled without sewing. In this project, bamboo skewers weave though pairs of signatures to hold the book together. Wrap a round bone piece in wire, threading small beads on wire while wrapping. Add beads to threads.

INSTRUCTIONS:

Paint skewers with black acrylic paint. Let dry.

Using a glue stick, cover one side of a piece of chipboard and center it on wrong side of cover paper. Press and smooth paper onto chipboard with a wad of waxed paper. Miter all four corners of cover paper with scissors, leaving excess equal to thickness of board. Apply glue stick to parallel sides of the cover paper and wrap securely over chipboard. Smooth with waxed paper. Repeat on remaining two sides. Set finished cover aside and repeat procedure for remaining cover.

On wrong (uncovered) side of chipboard, carefully measure halfway on the 8½" side and mark two 4¼" spots on cover. Make a score mark to bisect 8½" side on each cover. Fold in half with wrong sides together, but do not crease with bone folder. Lay hinge-cutting template on top of folded piece so fold is to left, under hinge measurement of template. Using a sharp awl, punch holes in cover, ½" in from fold as directed by template.

Designate one cover as front and one as back. On front cover, remove 2nd and 4th hinges with an X-Acto knife. On back cover remove 1st, 3rd and 5th hinges.

Using craft glue, glue two layers of front cover chipboard together. Do not glue hinge area since a hinge pin will be inserted to bind cover to signatures. Glue back cover layers together, also avoiding gluing hinge area.

Clip the edges with bulldog clamps while adhesive dries.

Serengeti Piano Hinge Book

SIZE: 4¹/₄" x 5¹/₂"

MATERIALS:
2 pieces 5¹/₂" x 8¹/₂" chipboard
2 pieces 7" x 10¹/₂" cover paper
11 bamboo skewers (hinge pins)
20 sheets 5¹/₂" x 8¹/₂" cardstock
  (4 each of 5 colors)

8 pieces of waxed linen thread,
  18" each (3 colors)
One hinge cutting template
One round African bone piece for
  cover embellishment
Various African bone beads - twining decoration
24" of 24 gauge black wire
Various small beads for wire embellishment

SUPPLIES:
Black acrylic paint • Glue stick • Scissors
• X-Acto knife • Awl • Wire cutters
• White craft glue • Waxed paper • 4 bulldog clips

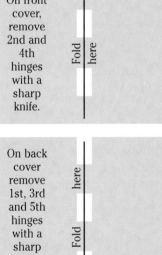

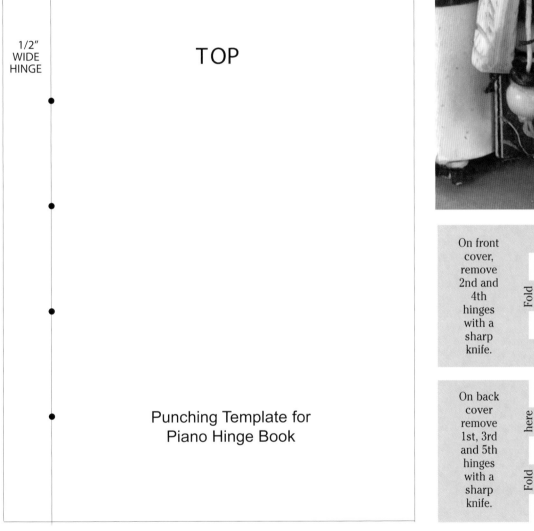

1/2" WIDE HINGE

TOP

Punching Template for
Piano Hinge Book

On front cover, remove 2nd and 4th hinges with a sharp knife. Fold here

On back cover remove 1st, 3rd and 5th hinges with a sharp knife. Fold here

1. Mark hinges on folded covers using template and an awl.
    Remove 2nd and 4th hinges on front cover. Remove 1st, 3rd and 5th on back cover.

2. Glue covers together using PVA glue, avoiding hinge area. Clamp and set aside to dry.

3. Fold cardstock sheets in half and nest in ten signatures of two sheets each.

Continued on page 42.

Continued from page 41.

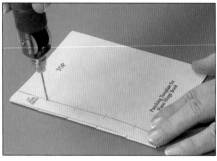

4. Mark top of signatures. Using template and awl, punch holes. Make a cut from spine to each hole.

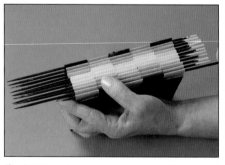

5. With signatures in order and beginning at front cover, thread skewers, connecting each signature to the next.

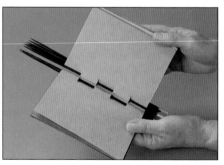

6. Correctly threaded, the book will now look like this inside.

Prepare text pages by folding each sheet of cardstock in half to 5¹/2" x 4¹/4". Do not use bone folder to crease folds. Nest cardstock together to make 10 signatures of two sheets each. Mark each signature with a T at top.

Using template and awl, mark holes in each signature. Make slits in spines from edge of the fold to points marked with awl. There will be four slits in each signature.

Decide color pattern for spine and put signatures in that order. Insert hinge pins, beginning with front cover and first sig-

nature. Line up hinges and gently fold back 1st, 3rd and 5th hinges of first signature.

Starting at bottom of spine, insert first skewer into cover hinge and thread to top using a gentle twisting motion. Leave about 1¹/2" of skewer showing at top of book.

Place second signature behind first and repeat procedure.

Continue until all signatures have been threaded, then add back cover. Double-check that skewers have not missed any hinges before moving on.

7. Twine threads to secure skewers at head and tail of book. Thread beads on tails and trim. Clip ends of skewers.

8. Wrap wire and thread beads onto cover piece. Adhere to cover.

Secure the Hinge Pins by Twining

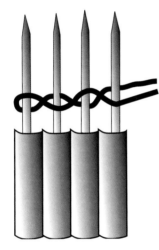

Find center of 18" length of waxed linen and loop it around top of last hinge pin. Cross threads between last pin and the one in front of it and repeat until you reach the front hinge pin.

The last step of making a piano hinge book involves securing the hinge pins by what's known as twining. Find center of 18" length of waxed linen and loop it around top of last hinge pin.

Cross threads between last pin and the one in front of it and repeat until you reach front hinge pin. Slide thread down each skewer until it touches top of book. Tighten thread and tie off with a square knot. Repeat twining with four more lengths of thread and tie each off with a square knot.

Twine three more rows of thread at bottom of book, this time twining from front of the book to back. When rows are completed, dab a little craft glue on inside of twining rows, including a small dot on knots. After glue dries completely snip bottom twining threads close to knots. Trim hinge pins using a pair of wire cutters or heavy duty clippers.

If desired, sand rough edges.

Wrap bone piece in wire, threading small beads on wire randomly while wrapping. Adhere to cover using hot glue or Quick Grab. Add bone beads to threads.

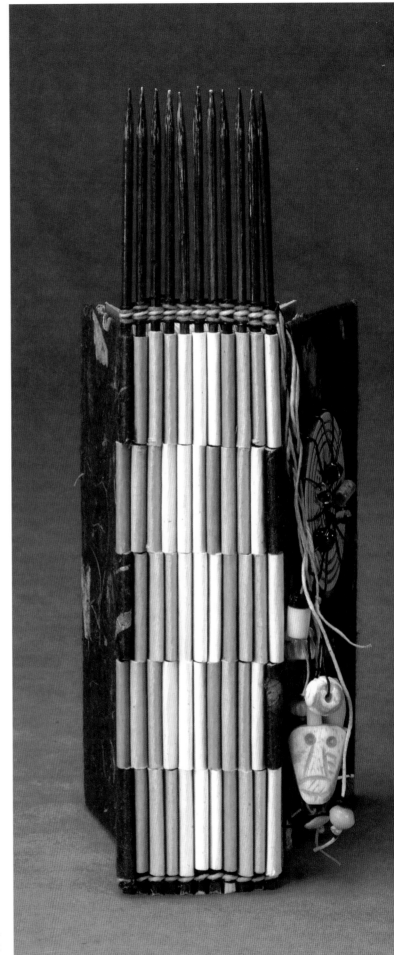

'Studio' Book with Clay Cover

Coptic stitch produces a lovely braided effect along the spine of the book. Covers may be made of virtually any material, from book board to wood to polymer clay.

SIZE: 3" X 4¹/₂"
MATERIALS:
1¹/₂ blocks Black Sculpey Clay
1 piece chip board 4¹/₂" x 3"
Baby powder
Tin Can Mail Studio stamp
Modern Options Copper Topper
Modern Options Patina Green
    Antiquing Solution

Metallic Rub-Ons
32 pieces text paper 4¹/₂" x 5³/₄"
4 pieces decorative paper for signature
    wraps 4¹/₂" x 4¹/₄"
1 piece cardstock for hole-punching tem
    plate 4¹/₂" square
3 pieces dark green waxed linen
    thread 24"
Krylon Matte Sealer

Cigar Box Cover by Lisa Renner
Clay Studio by M. K. Seckler

1. Roll out the clay on the thickest setting of pasta machine.

2. Trace template twice onto clay with craft knife. Mark holes with awl.

3. Sprinkle powder on stamp and impress into clay piece. Bake covers as directed.

*I*nside, text and decorative papers pages show just how luxurious these fabulous art books are.

SUPPLIES:
Pasta machine (optional) • Awl • Craft knife • Coffee stirrer • Sponge brushes or sea sponges • 1/16" hole punch • 6 binders' needles

Large 'Art' Book
SIZE: 4³/8" x 8¹/8"
MATERIALS:
Use a book board cover and appropriate size papers.

'Cigar Box Lid' Book
SIZE: 3¹/2" X 5¹/4"
MATERIALS:
Use a cigar box lid for the cover and appropriate size papers.

INSTRUCTIONS:
Make covers:

Mark 6 evenly spaced holes on one long side of chip board and punch three holes with a ¹/16" hole punch to create cover template. Set pasta machine on widest setting. After conditioning clay, run through machine and place on lightly powdered cutting board. Place template on clay and trim to size with craft knife.

Mark holes with awl. Remove template and enlarge holes with coffee stirrer. Repeat for front cover. Powder stamp and impress into clay. Press hard to get detail in stamp to show. Transfer both covers to cookie sheet and bake for 20 minutes in 275 degree oven. Cool completely.

Paint one side with Copper Topper paint and let dry completely. Paint another coat and dry to slightly tacky. Apply Patina Green while paint is still tacky. Let patina slowly develop, from an hour to several hours depending on humidity and ventilation. Repeat for other side of clay. When patina is fully developed on both sides, bring out detail of stamp with Metallic Rub-Ons.

Apply olive and dark bronze Rub-ons by gently smudging with fingertip.

Spray with a Krylon Matte Sealer to finish and allow covers to dry thoroughly.

Prepare signatures:

Fold 32 sheets of text paper in half to make sheets 4¹/2" x 2⁷/8". Nest paper in 8 groups of 4 sheets each. Mark a T in top right corner of each signature.

Fold decorative papers in half and wrap around four signatures. Fold cardstock in half and place fold next to one clay cover.

Mark holes on fold and mark top with a T to create hole-punching template. Nest template inside first signature with T of template matching T of signature.

Punch 6 holes according to template. Repeat for remaining 7 signatures.

Put signatures in order to be sewn.

4. Paint cooled clay with Copper Topper paint. Treat with Patina Green and allow to develop.

5. Bring out the detail of the stamp with metallic rub-ons.
Continued on page 46.

Sewing book:

Thread a needle onto each end of three pieces of waxed linen (6 total). Book will be sewn from back to front. Each thread will sew one pair of holes in book. Find midpoint of each thread and make a pinch. Place last signature on table face down, with holes facing you and T on your left facing up. Thread each needle pair through each pair of holes from inside signature so center of thread is in the middle of each pair of holes. You will have 6 needles hanging

outside at this point. To lock on back cover, place cover face down under last signature. Start with the thread on your right. Wrapping it around cover, thread needle through first hole in cover. Come up through hole and wrap thread according to (A). Repeat for second hole in pair and for remaining two pairs. In each pair of holes, threads should fall to inside of holes.

This will be true for all signatures until you lock on back cover.

To add a signature, be sure T is on your left facing up when stacked over previous one. Thread each needle into hole directly above it and back out opposite hole in pair (B.) Be careful not to pull too tightly. Thread should be snug but not so tight that it will pull or tear holes in signature. You want to be able to see the braid and if you pull too tightly, the braid will close up.

To secure signature, with first needle on right, skip one signature below and wrap thread according to (C), threading from right to left. The next needle will wrap in opposite direction, from left to right. Threads fall to center of holes.

Repeat for other two pairs of holes, being careful of thread tension.

Repeat steps for adding and securing signatures until crossover on last signature is complete. Place front cover on top of first signature.

Starting with first needle on right, wrap thread over cover and thread needle through first hole. Wrap around ascending thread going from right to left according to (D). Repeat for next hole in pair but wrap thread from left to right. Threads now fall to outside of holes. Repeat for each pair of holes.

To secure cover, skip down two signatures and wrap first thread on your right through ascending thread from right to left, and insert needle into first hole of first signature. Wrap second thread around ascending thread from left to right and insert needle into second hole of first signature. Tie off threads on inside with a square knot and clip threads to 1/4". Repeat procedure for remaining two pairs.

Continued from page 45.

6. Sew signatures, beginning at back cover.

7. Attach front cover.

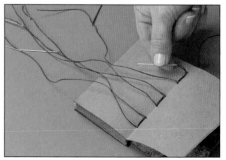

8. Secure cover by knotting threads in signature.

Sewing 'Studio' Books Together

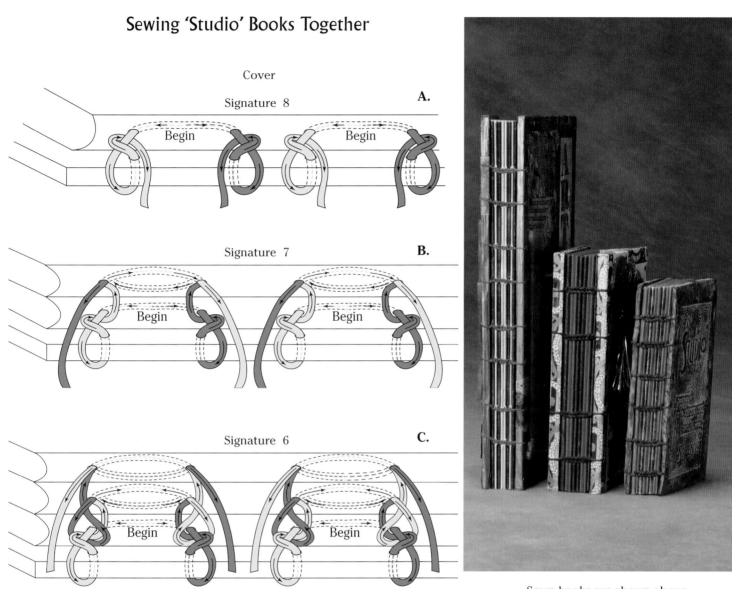

Cover

Signature 8

A.

Begin

Begin

Signature 7

B.

Begin

Begin

Signature 6

C.

Begin

Begin

Sewn books are shown above.

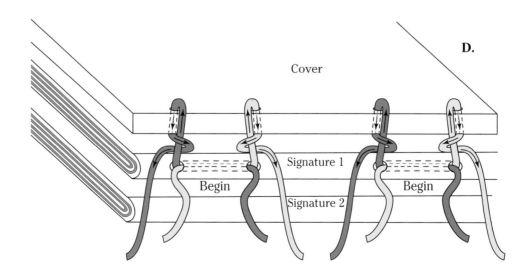

Cover

D.

Signature 1

Begin

Signature 2

Begin

*T*his book is designed to capture attention! Layers of paper create a narrowing tunnel effect that directs the focus toward your carefully chosen images.

French Tunnel Vision Book

SIZE: 3½" x 5"
MATERIALS:
2 pieces matboard 3½" x 5", one piece ½" x 5"
4 layers paper stock as follows:
    Layer 1, black 4¾" x 16"
    Layer 2, soft orange 4¾" x 18"
    Layer 3, brown 4¾" x 21"
    Layer 4, gray 4¾" x 25"
1 page antique French postcard art
1 piece brown spine cover paper 11" x 3"
1 punching template
4 bamboo skewers 4¾"
48" cream waxed linen thread

SUPPLIES:
Fibers • Beads • French postage stamps • Rubber Stamps (*Eclectic Omnibus* Paris, *Printworks* Fleur de Lis, *Treasure Cay* post, *Magenta* Fabrique' Par • Glue stick • PVA glue • Craft knife • Cutting mat • Metal ruler • Oval shape template with graduated sizes • Bone folder • Awl • Binder's needle • Bronze pigment ink pad • Brown dye ink pads

Create a surprise inside this beautiful book!

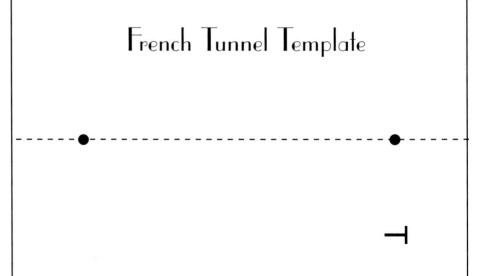

French Tunnel Template

INSTRUCTIONS:

Edge two cover pieces lightly with pigment ink and blot gently with paper towel as necessary. Let dry. • Fold each layer into eight-panel concertina by folding each sheet in half, quarters and eighths. Layers will be arranged with the widest panel (gray) at the back and the shortest (black) at the front. • Gray panel will not have holes cut in it. Set it aside.

Place black accordion fold in front of you so two end flaps are pointing away from you. Place 4" oval template centered over first valley fold and trace hole. Repeat for other two valley folds. Cut out holes. Repeat for other two accordion folds, using 3³/8" oval for the orange paper and 3" oval for brown paper.

Trim French postcards. Fold each in half vertically so image is centered on fold. Place first folded postcard in first valley fold, trimming to fit as necessary. Using a glue stick, adhere postcard to gray paper stock. Repeat for remaining two postcards.

Trim hole-punching template, score down the middle and fold with markings inside. Nest four panels, one inside the other, in order, with end flaps facing away from you: black followed by orange, then brown, then gray. Postcards should be visible through holes in the layers.

Turn entire assembly around so gray is in front. You will see four valley folds. Nest template with T in top right corner in first valley fold and punch two holes using an awl. Repeat for remaining three valley folds. Skewers will be sewn to fronts of four folds. Thread needle with waxed linen thread. Sew from inside fold, wrapping thread around skewer and returning needle through same hole.

Tie off with a square knot. Repeat for remaining 7 holes. Use glue stick to adhere four flaps to each other on each side.

Continued on page 50.

1. Fold each of the 4 layers into an 8-panel accordion.

2. Cut holes in the accordion panels with oval template.

3. Nest the layers.

4. Sew the panels together.

Tunnel Vision Book

Continued from page 49.

*T*his book is designed to capture attention! Layers of paper create a narrowing tunnel effect that directs the focus toward your carefully chosen images.

French Tunnel Vision Book

To make the cover, place 3" x 11" piece of brown paper vertically in front of you. Measure 5" from bottom and draw a horizontal line on the paper. Find midpoint of that line at 1¹/₂" and draw a vertical line from horizontal line to top of paper.

Apply PVA glue to spine piece and adhere it to brown paper. Center on vertical line with bottom of spine piece on horizontal line. Mark a ¹/₈" line to right and left of spine board. These spaces will be gutters. Apply PVA glue to paper to left of left gutter and place front cover board on vertical and horizontal lines, lining up with spine board. Repeat for back cover. Apply PVA glue to remaining strips above and below boards.

Fold over and press into place. Gently burnish with a wad of waxed paper, pressing gutters in gently. When cover assembly is dry, decorate cover with postage stamps and a few French rubber stamps.

Apply PVA glue to outside of left flap of postcard assembly. Nesting assembly inside cover for placement, adhere left flap to front cover. Repeat for right flap.

Thread fibers through spine and tie on outside with a square knot. Thread beads onto ends of fibers and knot. Add charms or other embellishments if desired.